AF478062

# Days of Purpose
# Days of Fulfillment

by

## Cheryl Gunsher

DEVORA PUBLISHING
JERUSALEM ◆ NEW YORK

*Days of Purpose, Days of Fulfillment*
Published by Devora Publishing Company
Text Copyright © 2007 by Cheryl Gunsher

COVER DESIGN: Benjie Herskowitz
ILLUSTRATOR: Cheryl Gunsher
TYPESETTING & BOOK DESIGN: Raphaël Freeman, Jerusalem Typesetting
EDITORS: Sandra Webb and Shirley Zauer
EDITORIAL & PRODUCTION MANAGER: Daniella Barak

Cover Artwork "The Healing of My Heart" by Cheryl Gunsher



Hard Cover ISBN: 978-1-932687-44-6

E-MAIL: sales@devorapublishing.com
WEB SITE: www.devorapublishing.com

Printed in the United States of America.

# Dedication

This book is dedicated to Rabbi Moshe Asher Boyarsky, the Magid of Vashilashok, may his memory be for a blessing. May the legacy of his Torah teachings continue to influence and inspire throughout the generations.

# Contents


Acknowledgements • ix
Introduction • xi

## Beginnings

A Rosh Hashanah Parable • 3
The Golden Fish • 5
A Special Place • 7
The Play • 9
Four Sons • 10
The Fortress • 12
A Foreign Land • 15
Symbols of Peace • 17
A Meeting • 18
The Radio • 20
Real Estate • 21
The Banquet Table • 22
The Reunion • 24
The True Servant • 26
The Garden • 28
A Hoary Crown • 30
The Circulatory System • 31
Dreamers • 33
The Human Race • 35
Wellsprings • 37
Wild Horses • 39
The Apartment • 41
Brothers • 43
Brothers, Revisited • 45
The Lost Treasure • 47

## Observations

Moments • 53
Opening Channels • 55
In the Right Direction • 57
Cotton Candy • 59
Hurt, Pain, and Anger • 61
Our Inner Teacher • 64
Marching Under the Banner of God • 66
Traveling on our True Paths • 68
Paying Attention • 70

## Meditations

Shabbat • 75
Clearing the Land • 76
Illumination • 78
Learning to Swim • 80
White Geese • 81
Flying Lessons • 83
Toward Freedom • 85

## Lessons

The Tapestry • 89
Sickness and Health • 91
From Love and With Love • 93
Your True Identity • 95
Your Holy Presence • 98
Hidden Treasures • 100
Thanksgiving • 102
The Seasoned Traveler • 104
Potentials • 106
Preparations • 108
Our Life's Blood • 110
Coal and Diamonds • 112
Will and Desire • 114
Arrogance • 116

The Flow of Our Lives • 118
The Baker • 120
A Voyage Through Rough Seas • 122
The Date Tree • 124
The Illuminating Light • 126
Searching for the Wind • 129
Eclipse • 131
Building Houses • 133
A Clear Path • 135
Coming Back • 137
Colors • 140
Dedication • 142

## New Beginnings

Walk Before Me and Be Perfect • 147
Willows by the Stream • 150
In Search of You • 152
The Caged Bird • 154
Awaiting the Dawn • 156
The Vineyard • 159
The Children of His House • 161
Trapped Within the Ice • 163
Transformation • 166
Birds in Flight • 169
Boundaries • 172
The Seed • 175
The Never-Ending Battle • 177
Elul • 180
Starting Over • 183
The Power of Love • 186
About the Author • 189

# Acknowledgments

With gratitude to my Lord and Master for all that He has given to me, and continues to give to me, every day of my life. I acknowledge, with thankfulness and appreciation, the gift of my healing and the guidance to live my life with purpose and fulfillment.

I acknowledge with recognition and thankfulness those individuals who God has sent into my life to help me in my journey. May God grant them blessing and success in their meaningful work:

To Meir Gunsher for his love, companionship and support.
To Dr. Herman Presby for his Torah teaching, guidance and encouragement.
To Reuven Ashenberg for his spiritual direction, encouragement and understanding.
To Sandra Webb for her editing talents, love and friendship.
To Sheryl Miller Kaye for her healing gifts, understanding and care.
To Dr. Paul Bahder for his advice, care and healing.
To Aaron Bar-David for his inspiration, insight and love.
To Aaron Gunsher for the many lessons that only a child can teach a parent. May you continue to grow in Torah and mitzvot and may you and your family merit God's blessing to fulfill the purpose of your lives.

# Introduction

*I will exalt You O Lord, my God, I cried out to You and You healed me.*

*Psalm 30:3*

*You have transformed my mourning into dancing; You undid my sackcloth and girded me with joy. Therefore my soul shall sing to You and not be silenced; my God forever will I thank You.*

*Psalm 30:12,13*

The sweet singer of Israel, King David, composed the book of Psalms. In this collection of writings we do not learn much historical detail about the events and circumstances of his life, but we do learn much about his response to them. Together with his many triumphs, King David had many struggles with illness, rebellions, losses and threats on his life; he faced great challenges, difficulties and disappointments.

Does King David ever give in to despair or give up on his salvation? Does he ever succumb to the tremendous trials he faced? Our reading of Psalms tells us this was not his way. He responds with action, with music, with meditation and most importantly with prayer. No matter how desperate the situation, he calls out to his God and pleads for help, understanding, forgiveness, strength and healing.

King David has demonstrated to us, by his example, the proper way to respond to the difficulties of life as well as to the successes, teaching us Who is the true Ruler of the world and from Whom true salvation comes. He has taught us never to give up hope no matter how trying the circumstances. These are powerful lessons for life, growth and the development of our souls.

The path of spiritual healing involves introspection, meditation, prayer, contemplation, Torah study, mitzvah observance, forgiveness and repentance. It involves an in-depth search of our souls. What motivates us? What activities do we involve ourselves in? What do we think about, dream about and yearn for? What are our hearts attracted to and how do we spend our precious time? What gives us joy? What causes us pain? What are our goals and what is our methodology for achieving them?

These are some of the important questions that, as spiritual seekers, we must explore. We must come to know our hearts, our resentments, our rigid thinking, our rote behaviors and our improper actions. To heal is to be free. We must leave the slavery of our negativity by recognizing and attaching ourselves to our true spiritual natures, and most importantly, to our God. We must strive to rid ourselves of the destructive and life-constricting thoughts, speech and behaviors that keep us from attaining spiritual greatness. Like our illustrious leader King David, we can reach out to our Lord and Master with contrite and broken hearts, yearning for His presence, His love and His salvation. Our Father in Heaven responds to heartfelt pleas, not only to those of a king, but to those of all of His children.

We must recognize our assets and our capabilities and know that when we cry out to our God, we will be heard. Our souls are our spiritual connections to our Creator and Master as well as our inner source of wisdom and guidance. When faced with illness, difficulty and challenge, like King David, we must open up our hearts to our true Source of help and salvation to heal our souls.

The writings in this book reflect my personal journey of spiritual healing. Through the methodologies of personal and formal prayer, Torah study and mitzvah observance, and meditative and contemplative writing, not only have I deepened my faith and trust in God, but I have strengthened my soul as well. The accumulated difficulties and pain that caused illness and sadness have been replaced by health and joy. The cure was not found in a bottle, but rather within the soul. Like King David, I cried out to my God and He healed me. Forever will I thank Him.

*Cheryl Gunsher*

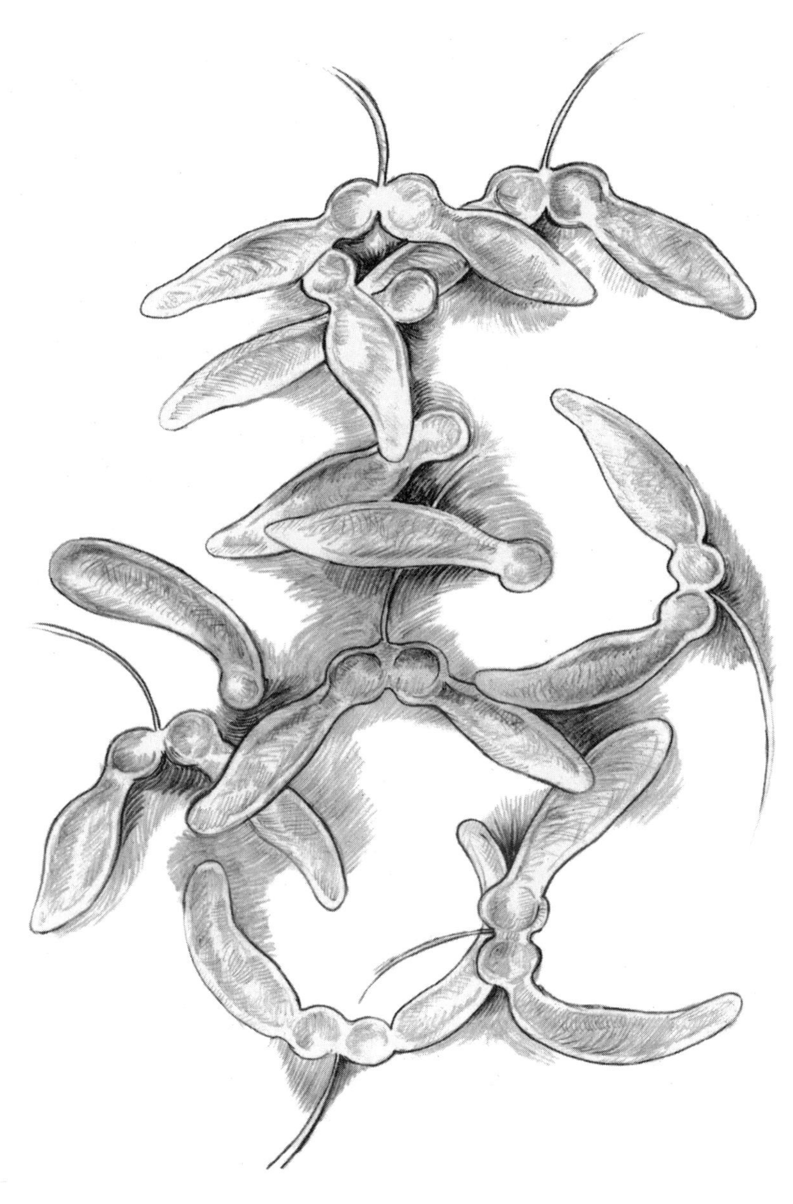

# Beginnings

# A Rosh Hashanah Parable

When the princess was born, her Father the King gave her a beautiful gown. It was exquisite in color and design and the little princess looked lovely wearing it. As she grew up, she understood that the gown was not hers to keep forever and that one day her Father would ask her to return it. In the meantime, her responsibility was to take good care of it. When there was a stain, she diligently cleaned it; when there was a rip, she mended it as soon as she could. But gradually, she became neglectful. It took her longer to make a repair. Sometimes she even decided that the stains weren't so bad and that no one would notice them anyway. Over time, she stopped even noticing the rips and stains, or acted as if she didn't even see them.

Her Father the King was truly distressed at how neglectful of her gown his daughter had become. He waited patiently for her to open her eyes and to remember her responsibility, and over the years offered her opportunities and reminders. But the kingdom offered so many distractions and diversions that she became accustomed to them and forgot what was expected of her as a daughter of the King.

Eventually, He came to tell her that it was time to return to Him the once beautiful gown. As soon as He asked for it, her eyes were opened to her shame and humiliation; she saw with clarity that her once-beautiful gown had become a rag. Distressed and upset, she begged her Father to give her time to clean and repair it. He told her that He had already given her much time and that there was no more time to give.

Knowing that her opportunities were gone, her sorrow was great. She realized that she had wasted the precious time her

Father had given her. She had ruined the exquisite gown, and she was no longer able to fix it.

May we never be in the position of the princess. May we take great care to guard the beautiful garments we have been given. May we use our time wisely and be ever-vigilant, so that we may return our garments in good condition. May we be mindful that our Father in Heaven may come at any time to reclaim them. In these days of repentance, may our eyes be open to whatever stains and rips we see in them. May our efforts be diligent to clean and repair them so that we may not suffer the shame of having to face our Father with a rag in our hands and sorrow in our hearts. Amen.

# The Golden Fish

The Village was located at the very edge of the Kingdom, bordering the great ocean. It was the poorest of all the towns and villages in the Kingdom: The barren land was full of rocks, and the people of the Village could not raise crops in its soil. Even worse for the villagers was that the ocean bordering their village was frozen. No one could remember how or when it had happened, but the ocean was covered with a thick, impenetrable layer of ice. This icy barrier prevented the people from fishing, thus making an important food source unavailable to them.

The King, distressed at the plight of the villagers, decided to send for His Minstrel, a man who traveled throughout the Kingdom, singing his songs and gladdening the hearts of all who heard him. The King sent the Minstrel to be His messenger and to travel down to the Village with the frozen ocean. When the Messenger arrived and saw the poverty and the despair of the villagers, his heart was saddened and he was unable to sing his sweet songs. He felt the hunger and depression that surrounded him and saw the ice that covered over the blue ocean. He left the Village with a heavy heart.

The Minstrel began traveling throughout the Kingdom, not to sing, but to publicize the plight of the villagers and to arouse compassion in the hearts of the people. He asked that at the end of the upcoming festival days, they travel at nightfall to the Village with the frozen ocean. He told them each to come with a glad heart, a smile, and a candle.

When the festival days ended, men, women, and children from all over the Kingdom began their journey to the Village in a remote part of their country. They came singing songs, with gladness in their hearts, smiles on their faces, and candles, just as the

King's Messenger had asked them. They came with the sincere wish of sharing with their less-fortunate country people the joy that they had experienced during the festival days.

The people gathered on the shore, facing the ocean. They lit their candles and smiled, feeling the happiness of helping the villagers in their hearts. Their many separate flames came together to form one great flame, and soon, droplets pooled on the icy surface, and then the water started rippling forth in waves. The King's Messenger took a net and threw it into the ocean and brought out a golden fish. The fish glittered and shone in the reflection of the great flame. The villagers were overjoyed when they saw the golden fish because they knew now that their ocean contained life. They would no longer be hungry, and they had hope for the future.

The King was greatly pleased with His Messenger and with the people of the Kingdom. He declared that from then on the melting of the ocean would be commemorated in the Village every year at the end of the festival days. Even though the people did not remember how the ocean had originally become frozen, the King wanted them to remember forever how it had melted.

# A Special Place

The King sent two of his beloved sons on a journey, each with his own unique path. One son was sent on a path where there were guides who directed him on his way and provided him with maps and a Guidebook. They sent him on trails that had been well traveled. He was instructed about how to avoid the dangers of the forest, how to climb steep mountains, and how to navigate rough waters. He was warned of the many obstacles, traps, and pitfalls he would encounter along the way.

During his journey, he accomplished many things and traveled far. He composed his own guidebooks and drew his own maps for those who would follow him. As he neared the end of his journey, admirers gathered to praise him and all that he had achieved. His time had been well spent, and his Father the King was proud of his son's many accomplishments.

The journey of the other son was much different from that of the first. He was not given his brother's advantages. He received neither Guidebook nor maps and there were no guides to help him on his way. Much of his time was lost in wrong turns and pursuing paths that turned into dead ends. He often found himself enveloped in a deep fog that obscured his vision, and he became battered and bruised from the obstacles and traps that he could not see and had not anticipated. At times he became lost in mazes of confusion and despaired of ever finding his way back to his Father.

Although the son was not always aware of it, his Father was close by to help and to encourage him. His Father never deserted him and watched over his every step. Whenever the son felt overwhelmed by pain and distress, he called out to his Father, and He responded with comfort and healing. With his Father's encouragement, he was able to strengthen himself and to find his way back to the right path.

At the end of his journey, this son had neither admirers to praise him nor guidebooks and maps of his own. His heart was full of sorrow and shame for all the time he had wasted in confusion and despair. Although he had overcome many obstacles and had painstakingly found his way back from his wrong turns, he was aggrieved to think of all the time he had lost. He knew that his brother's days had been full and productive, and he felt ashamed of his own lack of accomplishment.

Yet the King was as proud of this son as He was of His other son. He was well aware of all the hardships that His son had overcome. Knowing the hearts of all His children, He knew the sadness that His son felt. To show him and all of His Kingdom how beloved he was to Him, He honored him with a special place in His Court, a place where no one else, not even His other beloved son, could stand.

The King understood the depths of His son's suffering and knew that through His son's broken heart shone the light of love. For such a son, there would always be a special place in the Kingdom of his Father.

# The Play

*She asked, "Tell me, my friend, why do I suffer so?"*
*"I don't know," I said, "but please let me share my story*
*with you."*

Your Father has given you a part in His great play. You have not seen the beginning of the play, and you do not know what will happen after you leave the stage. Your part is a small one, and compared to the overall length of the play, it will go by very quickly. You have not been provided with a script, and are unsure how to play your part. You may be puzzled as to why you are sharing the stage with particular actors, and why you have been placed in certain scenes. You may wonder why it seems that your part is more difficult than that of other actors.

Just know this, my friend. Your Father has given you a great opportunity, and although your part is a small one, it can affect the outcome of the entire production. Your role is important and you have the tremendous responsibility of giving the best performance that you can. Be mindful that the most beloved of your Father's children are given the most difficult parts to play.

No, my friend, I can't tell you why you suffer. Our perspective is narrow and we are not given the ability to see beyond the limitations of our hearts and minds. We must trust that our Father, who knows all and sees all, is directing this production for our benefit and out of His great love for His children. In your time of suffering, remember that love, and call out to Him for help and guidance. Your Father will always respond and will never forsake you.

"I think," she said, "that my suffering has brought me closer to my Father. Perhaps that is the reason for my suffering."

"Perhaps," I said.

# Four Sons

The King sent His four sons on a trip through His forest. He equipped each one with a Guidebook, a shovel, a candle, and a basket.

The first son loved to travel through the forest: Restless and easily distracted, he was unable to stay in one place for long, and was always looking for new paths and adventures. He hardly ever glanced at his Guidebook, and when he returned to his Father, his basket was empty.

The second son also loved to travel, but lingered at places that caught his eye. Along the way, he collected whatever he could find easily – wildflowers, leaves, and twigs; he rarely used his shovel. He occasionally consulted his Guidebook, but he didn't consider himself much of a student, and gave up studying it whenever he found it difficult to understand. When he returned to His Father, his basket was full, but it contained little of value.

The third son did not travel as much as his two older brothers. Rather, he spent a long time at each place he came to, and spent much time studying his Guidebook, realizing its great importance. He came to understand that hidden in the forest were precious stones, and that finding them would require great effort and concentration. He used his shovel to dig for them and his candle to illuminate the way. He was not always able to discern the difference between precious stones and those of lesser value. Sometimes he lost his way or wasted time, distracted by the forest's many diversions. However, as soon as he became aware of his error, he would find his way back to the correct path. When he returned to his Father, his basket contained a mixture of precious stones and stones of lesser value.

The fourth son understood that every moment was valuable,

and traveled only when it was necessary. He didn't want to take time away from studying his Guidebook or searching for precious stones. He was single-minded and focused on his task, paying no attention to the diversions that had distracted his brothers. He understood the importance of the shovel his Father had given him and spent long periods digging and searching. He kept his candle always lit, and used it to explore all the corners and hard-to-reach places that could only be found through painstaking diligence. When he returned to his Father, his basket was full of precious stones.

May we be single-minded in our task.

May we be diligent and focused.

May we have the merit of returning to our Father with a basket full of precious stones. Amen.

# The Fortress

The King sent His daughter to live with adoptive parents in one of the cities in His Kingdom, expecting them to love and care for her. However, the adoptive couple was preoccupied with their own conflicts and arguments and neglected the princess and her needs. For years she watched anxiously as they hurt each other with harsh words and uncontrolled anger. Finally, when she felt she could no longer live in a place where she could find no peace, the princess fled from her adoptive home to the King's forest. There her Father protected her and kept her safe for many years.

One day, a young woman who had known the princess as a child was walking in the forest. She came upon a great fortress around which a fierce battle was taking place. Soldiers with catapults were hurling stones at the fortress and trying to breach its sturdy ramparts with battering rams. As soon as a hole was made in the fortress wall, defending soldiers arrived and worked furiously to repair the damage.

The young woman watched for a long time, transfixed by the scene, wanting neither to leave nor to draw any closer. An elderly man with poor eyesight who was passing by asked her what she was looking at. She described the battle scene and the great fortress that was under attack. He asked her if she knew what was inside the fortress. The question surprised her: She had been so absorbed in watching the battle that she hadn't considered what it was that the soldiers were so intent on trying to capture. The young woman told him she didn't know the answer to his question. The elderly man said that he felt it was important for her to find out what was inside the fortress, and that despite the danger, she should find a way in.

She agreed, and pushing aside her fears, she stealthily made her way toward the fortress. Amid the constant assault that was going on around her, she made it safely to the great gate that led to the door. She opened the door and entered. Once she was inside, she was amazed to realize that the fortress had no walls, no ceilings, no floors, no rooms, and no furniture. Within was a dense white light, and the only person to be found was a young girl sitting sadly by herself, her knees tucked up to her chest and her arms wrapped around them. Her head was bent over her knees, and she looked very lonely. The young woman had found the princess.

Without ever exchanging a word, the young woman knew that the girl wanted very much for the walls of the fortress to come down, to be freed from her safe but isolated existence. She knew it was too dangerous to try to rescue the girl while the battle was still raging, but she vowed to herself that one day she would come back. She would not forget the girl's plight.

Years passed, and although the woman suffered with the knowledge that the girl was still not free, she knew that the battle was not yet over. The adoptive parents passed away, and the woman, who had known them well, went to visit their graves. As she stood there, she thought sadly of their many years of arguing, and of all the time that they had spent hurting each other and the princess. She felt sorrow in her heart at the wasted years of their lives, years that could have been spent in love instead of in bitterness, years that could have been devoted to serving the King instead of serving the cause of misery and strife. The woman hoped that perhaps they now had the peace that had eluded them during their lifetime. She walked away from the graves with a sense of freedom from the constrictions and burdens of the past.

She knew that the battle was now over, and that it was safe to return to the fortress in the forest. She found her way back to it and discovered that there were no longer any soldiers, catapults, or battering rams. She went through the gate and opened the door. The princess was still sitting in exactly the same position that she had been in years before. The woman walked over to her, bent down, and helped the princess to her feet. With her arm around the princess, the woman and the girl walked out of the fortress together.

# A Foreign Land

The King sent his son to live temporarily in a foreign land. The King told him that his new life would be very different from the one that he had known in his Father's palace. In this new land, he would have to work: There would be different kinds of work that he could choose, and the type of work he chose would determine the kind of payment he received. For some kinds of work, he would be paid in the currency of the foreign land; for others, he would be paid in the royal currency of the King. He was told that the two currencies were not interchangeable, and that he would not be able to bring the foreign currency back with him to the palace when he returned.

The prince found life in the new land to be one of hardship. He had to start working at a young age and was paid in foreign currency. He knew that working was important to take care of his needs, yet even after those needs had been met, he continued working – not for what was necessary but for those things that had become attractive to him. Soon he was spending all of his time earning wages in foreign currency.

Days passed quickly into years, and as the prince became accustomed to the ways of the foreign land, he forgot what life had been like in the palace, his true home. From time to time he received letters from his Father reminding him of what he needed to accomplish, but the prince left the letters in his mailbox, unopened.

The time for the prince to return home was now approaching. His Father sent him an urgent letter by special delivery, and this time the prince opened it. The message notified him that he would soon be leaving the foreign land, and reminded him that all of the foreign currency he had accumulated would have to be left behind.

The prince became distressed. He knew that he had been so preoccupied with work that paid him in foreign currency that he had spent no time at tasks that would pay royal wages. He didn't even know what kind of work it was that paid royal wages! He was depressed at the thought of returning to his Father as a pauper, but he had become so stuck in his habits in the foreign land that he felt he couldn't change. Even knowing that he would soon have to return to his Father empty-handed, the prince chose to spend his remaining days working for things that had no lasting value.

May we be mindful of the important work we must do.

May we be diligent in accomplishing our work.

May we have the merit of returning to our Father with wealth and pride rather than with poverty and shame. Amen.

# Symbols of Peace

The bird is not subject to the traps and pitfalls of earthbound creatures; it escapes predators by flying freely beyond their grasp. With the quick and graceful movements of its wings, the bird finds refuge in the vast and open sky. Without borders or boundaries, its path of escape is limitless. Free of oppression and entrapment, the bird can soar toward the heavens.

Peace comes through freedom.

The pot holds its contents safely inside, protecting them from spilling out and becoming lost. The pot shields its contents from the destructiveness of fire: It keeps together what it holds inside. The material of the pot forms the boundaries that safeguard its contents, preventing them from being consumed.

Peace comes through security.

The river's current follows its own particular course, the way it is meant to go. You can take a raft and ride this current, following its path, curves, and turns. The course may be rocky or smooth, but it will always go its own way. You may want to jump off the raft and fight the current, trying to swim upstream, but the river will overpower you. Tranquility comes only through accepting the direction of the river, no matter where it takes you. Whether its path leads over rapids, through narrow paths, or between great mountains, you must stay on your raft and follow the course of your journey.

Peace comes through acceptance.

# A Meeting

You have been given the great privilege of meeting with your Father the King. Do not rush into this meeting unprepared. Ready yourself to make the most of your time in His presence. Clear your mind of the extraneous thoughts that divert your attention. Open the gateway of your heart to receive whatever expressions of love, advice, or encouragement your Father may bestow upon you. Concentrate on the words that you will speak, ever mindful of with Whom you will be speaking. With great anticipation and trepidation, enter His royal chambers.

If you have prepared yourself properly, you may feel the light of His presence. You may be granted the great opportunity of connecting your small candle to His great flame. Approach your Father with all your heart's desire. Speak to Him from the strength of your will and the determination of your soul. Think of this meeting as if it were your only opportunity to stand in your Father's presence. Lose your concept of time in this timeless encounter. Ask for His advice. Ask for His comfort. Ask for His love. Ask for permission to come closer to Him. Although you may not feel worthy, and even though you have often strayed from the path that He has set for you, know that your Father wants you to come closer to Him. For each step you make, He will respond with help and encouragement. Know that each meeting with your Father is precious, so use this time wisely.

It may be hard to leave your Father's royal chambers, but when you do so, do not rush from this meeting. Do not run to the tasks that await you, but rather, take time first to absorb the spiritual nourishment that you have received. Make the transition from His royal chambers to your life outside the palace a gradual one.

Use the strength of your Father's love, and let it strengthen you when you are no longer standing before Him. Be aware that wherever you are in His kingdom, He is always watching over you.

# The Radio

Wisdom emanates from our souls like radio waves, which carry their messages through the air: Unless we are tuned in, we won't be able to hear it. To be able to receive this broadcast, we have to get rid of static and increase the volume. Our minds have so many different broadcasts coming through all the time that we have to adjust our receivers to receive the messages from our souls. We must quiet our minds in order to become receptive to the important information continuously being sent to us.

Our souls are our link to God's wisdom. They are both the vitalizing force of our being and our connection to the divine understanding embodied by our Creator. Our souls are the small flames that connect us to the great and holy fire of their Source. To receive this wisdom, we need silence: All other channels must be stilled. By silencing our minds, we will be able to accept the lessons that our souls have to teach us.

Quieting our minds is not an easy task. Tuning in and being receptive to these broadcasts takes practice. However, our efforts will be greatly rewarded because they inevitably lead to an enhanced understanding of who we are and of our individual paths. Let us endeavor to learn the secrets that our divine transmitters are sending us by opening the channel that will bring us closer to the Source of all wisdom.

# Real Estate

Her house was in disrepair: Pipes were breaking, water was leaking, floorboards were splitting, the roof was falling in. Everywhere she looked there were cracks and holes. As soon as one repair was made, something else would come apart. It truly seemed as if the house would collapse from all the strain and tension. Despite the overwhelming task ahead of her, she worked hard little by little, bit by bit.

After much effort, the balance finally began to shift. More parts of the house were in working order than were those that needed fixing. Although some parts were still breaking down, many were now working properly. However, progress was slow and uneven, and there were many setbacks and disappointments. She continued to work with determination, always supported by her Father.

Eventually, the house was fully restored. In her happiness, she thanked her Father for all His help and encouragement. Her Father sent her a message telling her that now that her house was whole and stable, it was time for her to move to the new and more spacious house that He would provide for her.

Until now, she had had to spend so much time just keeping her old house from falling apart that she had had no time to expand or renovate. Now it was time for true growth and development. Without the pressures and challenges of constant repairs, she would have the opportunity of living comfortably in a stable and spacious structure. The energy and determination that she had put into her old house were freed up and now she could create rather than repair. She rejoiced at the new beginning, and filled with the joy of freedom and anticipation, she gave thanks to her Father for the great gift of a new house.

# The Banquet Table

As she approached the King's mansion, the caretaker warmly welcomed her inside. He graciously ushered her through its many corridors and hallways and into the main dining room. She was amazed by the long banquet table, filled from one end to the other with delicious food. There were fresh fruit and vegetables of every color and texture; meats, fish, grains, and breads of every description; pies, puddings, desserts, wines, teas, and beverages in abundance. The sights and smells were a delight to the senses.

The caretaker invited her to partake of this feast. He told her that everything on the table was for her, and that she could eat as much as she liked. Until that moment she hadn't realized how hungry she was. In fact, she had been at the edge of starvation for years but had become so accustomed to her hunger that she hadn't been aware of how deprived she had been. However, much to the surprise of the caretaker, she ran from the banquet table without touching any of the food, and out of the mansion as quickly as she could.

The sight of such abundance had made her realize the extent of her deprivation. If there was so much nourishing and life-sustaining food in the world, why had she gone hungry for so long? She was overwhelmed by the realization that there was an abundance of food in the world that until now had never been available to her. She felt deeply saddened.

After some time had passed, she was able to go back to the mansion. The caretaker taught her how to eat healthily and with enjoyment, and over time, to accept the feast she was offered and to be strengthened by its nourishment.

Week after week, she returned to the mansion, and she became healthy and strong. She offered heartfelt thanks to the King for providing her with this opportunity for growth and healing, and to the caretaker for his help and encouragement. The King accepted her gratitude and bestowed on her the position of caretaker of another of His many mansions. He knew that her struggles had taught her both how to partake of His bountiful feast and how to feed and strengthen others who were hungry. She accepted the position humbly and gratefully, and spent the remainder of her days as a caretaker in the service of her King.

# The Reunion

His Father the King had sent the prince to a foreign land to accomplish an important mission, but the prince found it difficult to be away from his Father, and yearned to live within the palace walls, close to Him. The prince knew that he had to fulfill his mission before he could return home to the palace, but the separation from his Father was hard for him to endure.

The King supplied his son with a Guidebook containing directives on how to conduct himself during his time away from the palace. The Guidebook detailed how to eat, to dress, to speak, and to act. The prince knew that if he strayed from the directives that his Father had set forth for him, he would be unable to accomplish his mission successfully.

The King instructed his son to call Him at least three times a day to maintain his connection with his Father in this distant land. He told the prince to keep reminders on his body and clothes, and throughout his dwelling, so that he would not forget his true home, his true identity, or his true Father.

Keeping connected to his Father and following his Father's directives was difficult in this foreign land because the customs and habits of most of the residents were different from the ways of his Father. It was a place of confusion where the very existence of the King was often denied. Many had forgotten their King and kept almost no connection to Him.

The prince nevertheless continued his attachment to his Father, contemplating the reminders and faithfully studying his Guidebook. Reading his Father's words comforted and reassured him of his Father's love and concern and he talked to his Father often, despite the distance that separated them. The prince understood that if even one day passed without his thinking about his Father, he would become confused, as had so many of the foreign residents. He knew it was vital to keep his connection to his Father's directives because without them he would surely become lost.

The King took pride in this son who had not forgotten his Father and who had faithfully followed His directives. When it came time for the prince to return to the palace, everyone in the King's court celebrated the reunion of the devoted, loyal son and his proud and loving Father.

# The True Servant

Many people thought that as the adopted son of the emperor, the prince lived a charmed life: Surely, living among the wealthy, powerful, and privileged of the emperor's palace was a position to be envied. In contrast to the prince's luxurious lifestyle was the oppressed existence of his people, whose lives were bitter and full of hardship because of the cruel subjugation inflicted on them by merciless taskmasters. Although outwardly the prince seemed to have a life of ease, comfort, and freedom, the truth was that no one suffered more inwardly from his enslavement than did the prince.

The adopted prince had grown up in the pagan environment of the emperor's palace, surrounded by idolatry and falsehood. Separated from his true family, and living at the very center of degradation and impurity, his soul had had to fight constantly against his toxic surroundings. Daily he had been assaulted by the debased customs and improper dress that were common within the palace walls. Although physical subjugation afflicted the bodies of his people, their spiritual solidarity allowed them to distance their souls from the foreign ways of their oppressors in a way the prince could not.

By living apart from them and his true family, the prince had had an isolated existence, unable to derive either support or strength from their nurturing and life-sustaining ways. Cut off from his true heritage, the prince's eyes had endured the sight of idols, his ears the sounds of idolatrous speech. His pure heart, which yearned for truth, had been surrounded by falsehood. His enslavement was the harshest of all.

Once he had grown to manhood, the prince could no longer tolerate the poisonous atmosphere of the palace, and he had fled, becoming a wanderer. Disconnected from his people and with no permanent home, he lived as a stranger, a sojourner among foreign peoples with foreign customs in foreign lands. Yet the prince never forgot his people during his many years in exile, and his true Father in Heaven never forgot the prince.

His Father the King had watched over him throughout the years that he had lived in the emperor's palace, and had protected him during his wanderings. The King was preparing his son to redeem his people. The trials that the prince had withstood – the idolatrous environment of the emperor's palace, the alienation of being a stranger and wanderer among nations – had served him well, preparing and strengthening him for the great challenges that awaited him.

Despite the confidence his Father placed in him, the prince felt inadequate and undeserving. Surely, he thought, others were more qualified than he to lead his people. However, in the eyes of his Father, the prince's misgivings only further proved his worthiness. His Father knew that the prince had learned the painful lessons of his enslavement and exile. Through his trials and sufferings, the prince had elevated himself from the darkness of oppression to the light of freedom, from the degradation of the emperor's palace to the splendor of the King's court. The prince was now prepared to be the redeemer of his people, to lead them out of the land of their enslavement to serve their Father in freedom. Through his hardships, the prince had earned the merit of being a true servant of his Father the King.

May we merit witnessing the final redemption speedily in our days. Amen.

# The Garden

The garden was overrun with weeds, deeply rooted and tall. Full of stones, the earth beneath was barren, unable to receive the light of the sun because of the debris that covered it. Many wild animals had come to claim their part of this overgrown and neglected land.

As a child, the princess had planted seeds in this soil, but nothing had grown there. She was told that before her birth, the now-desolate land had been a thriving garden with tall, strong trees. Lush meadows of flowers had once surrounded it. It saddened the young princess to think of how barren the garden had become.

The garden had been a family inheritance for many generations, but the princess' family had neglected it. They neither appreciated its beauty nor understood its value. They had allowed the once-productive garden to become a wasteland. Their ancestors had worked hard and tirelessly to develop its potential, but their children had abandoned their precious inheritance. Their neglect had allowed the dissipation of the great wealth entrusted to them.

Unlike the rest of her family, the young princess understood the value of her inheritance. She knew that underneath the weeds and rocks was a rich and fertile soil with great potential. For years she worked alone, clearing the rocks, uprooting the weeds, and restoring the land. After much hard work, the soil was again able to receive the light of the sun.

As the princess grew to womanhood, she realized that her life's work was restoration of the land. Although she had put much effort into preparing the soil for planting and making it again suitable to support life and growth, she came to understand that it was not her job to restore the garden to its former glory. she was only clearing the way for a successor who would develop the land and make it truly productive.

The princess asked her Father the King to send her an heir, a child who would appreciate his inheritance and care for it properly. The King, pleased with the princess' request, sent her a son capable of continuing the work of restoring the garden. The princess taught her son to love the land as she did, and to work tirelessly at planting, cultivating, and protecting their precious inheritance.

As the child grew, the princess saw that her son had a great love and appreciation of the land. The princess knew that she could entrust him with the responsibility of building up the garden to flourish as it had during the time of their ancestors. The young prince felt proud and humble to be given this great responsibility. He prayed to the King to give him the strength and wisdom to be able to fulfill his mother's dreams. The King heard his prayers and granted his request. The great treasure that had been lost was restored. Once again, with the blessings and encouragement of the King, the garden thrived and blossomed, bringing new life to the fertile and holy soil.

May we merit to witness the restoration and reclamation of all the neglected gardens in the world speedily in our days. Amen.

# A Hoary Crown

The hair of youth is colored and flexible; the individual strands are not as deeply rooted and may be easily pulled out. With maturity the strands become brittle, lose color, and become more deeply rooted in the skin.

Similarly, as we age we accustom ourselves to patterns of behavior that become habitual. All behavior becomes ingrained and is not easily uprooted, whether positive, or God forbid, negative. White hair does not bend as easily as does the colored hair of youth.

The time to establish proper behavior is early in life when, like our hair, we are pliable and can be more easily molded and shaped. If we don't pluck out the negative traits of youth, they will become firmly rooted and resistant to change.

It is difficult with less flexible material both to repent of sins that have become entrenched with age, and to establish positive behavior. This process of repenting of our negative traits and of perfecting our positive traits needs to begin early in life and to become a lifelong endeavor. Delaying this work only makes it more difficult.

At this time of repentance, let us pray that the white hairs we develop with age may represent a lifetime of positive behavior that we have been diligent in perfecting. Let us pray that our hair may become a crown of accomplishments, one that frames our heads with the wisdom of a lifetime of unbending devotion to Torah and *mitzvot*.

May we never know the shame of wearing the worthless crown of a lifetime spent in emptiness and vanity. Amen.

# The Circulatory System

Our hearts are vital pumps that keep our bodies functioning; our arteries are the channels that carry this life-sustaining blood. Just as the circulation of blood nourishes our bodies, so does the life-blood of love sustain our spiritual lives.

Our spiritual hearts send forth and receive the love that sustains our souls. Damaged and blocked arteries disrupt the flow of blood through our bodies. Similarly do anger, resentment, and jealousy toward others disrupt the flow of love through our souls. The spiritual channels become blocked, leaving the soul with an inadequate supply of soul-sustaining love. The remedy for this illness is the medicine of forgiveness.

The first letter of *selihot* (forgiveness) is a *sameh*, a circular letter symbolizing the proper functioning of our spiritual circulatory systems. Forgiveness keeps the channels open, allowing love to flow unimpeded. If, God forbid, we let anger and resentments build up, our ability to love becomes impaired and we become unable to fulfill properly the mitzvot of loving God and of loving our neighbors. We damage our spiritual health by constricting the flow of spiritually nourishing love: a heart that cannot send forth love will also be unable to receive love.

To receive forgiveness from God, we need to initiate the process by forgiving others. When we work to clear up the resentments and anger that we harbor in our hearts, God will respond by opening up the channels of His love and forgiveness to us. As we remove the barriers of the evil inclination from our hearts, God allows us to move closer to Him and to be strengthened by His love.

Before we ask God to forgive us, we must first begin the

process of repentance ourselves by clearing out all the bitterness and resentment that have found a home in our hearts. We need to search our hearts for those obstacles that keep us from truly fulfilling the mitzvah of loving kindness.

As we search for leaven on Passover, let us also search our hearts thoroughly, looking for every last crumb of anger. Only after we have completed a thorough inspection can we then turn to God and pray that He opens our hearts to His love, His mercy, and His loving kindness.

May God's love strengthen and sustain us in this coming year, and may our prayers be answered. Amen.

# Dreamers

While we sleep, the images of our dreamlike state seem true: Even our most fantastic adventures appear real to us. As soon as we awaken, however, we realize that our dreams were but the workings of our imagination. Similarly, during a time of exile, when we believe in the deceptions of our material existence instead of the truth of our hidden spiritual reality, we become as confused as dreamers, mixing elements of truth and falsehood.

Our sins derive from an acceptance of this dreamlike existence. In this state we may, God forbid, misperceive. We may mistakenly believe that God has abandoned and left us unprotected against our enemies. We may envy the worldly prosperity of the wicked. We may also misunderstand the suffering of the righteous people, failing to comprehend the great love that God has for those who are faithful to Him.

During the time of our exile, the *tzadikim*, the righteous people, have shed many tears as they diligently worked in the fields of Torah and mitzvot. They wept not from personal sorrow but for those among their people who perceived only the surface of the world. They wept for those who lived as dreamers, unaware of the hidden bounty lying in the fertile fields of Torah.

The tzadikim also cried tears of joy when they contemplated the time to come, when their efforts would bring forth a bountiful harvest and the world would acknowledge and bless both the workers and their Master. Then will be made visible the harvest that was growing, hidden from view, during our exile. What was concealed will shine forth as a new light to be enjoyed by the tzadikim who toiled in the garden of Torah. Through them, the world will be nourished with an abundant harvest that will spread the light of Torah throughout the world. Then will we awaken from the slumber of exile to the revelation of the redemption, and be dreamers no more.

# The Human Race

The spectators applauded as the runners approached the finish line, cheering most loudly for those in the lead. They knew that these athletes had brought themselves to the forefront through sustained effort, rigorous training, and great diligence. The audience appreciated the perseverance and endurance that had been necessary to achieve a winning place in this difficult race.

The King had also watched the race, but from a vantage point different from the spectators'. From the perspective of His great palace overlooking the racecourse, He had viewed the race from start to finish. The spectators at the finish line did not know that the course of each runner had not been the same. Some runners had had paths with more obstacles than others, full of rocks and other obstructions difficult to navigate; some had had paths that were smooth and clear. The terrain for each had been different, too. Some had run on a level surface; others had struggled up and down hills. Some runners had negotiated courses with turns and detours; others had been on paths mostly straight. Some athletes had been given experienced coaches to guide and to encourage them through the many complexities of the racecourse. They had also benefited from training manuals and course maps to help them anticipate and prepare for unexpected difficulties.

In addition to the variation in courses that the athletes had encountered, each had also received supplies of varying quality. Some had been given durable footwear and warm outfits to protect them from rough terrain and inclement weather; others had lacked proper supplies and had become bruised and ill. Some athletes had had to run when they were hungry because they had not been provided with adequate nourishment; others had had to overcome low energy levels and the draining, constant demands of the race.

Each athlete had also started the race at a different point. Some had been given advantages that had offered them a head start, whereas others had had to start the race far behind the others.

At the conclusion of the race, when the King came forward to award prizes to the runners for their efforts, the spectators were puzzled. Even though they had seen the order in which the runners had crossed the finish line, it seemed that the King was awarding the prizes differently: Athletes who had crossed the finish line far behind the frontrunners also received great rewards from the King. The spectators realized that their perspective had been limited, and that only their wise and all-knowing King could truly evaluate the performances of the athletes. They joined their King in applauding the runners who had overcome obstacles and difficulties and persevered to finish the race in good standing.

May we have the wisdom to refrain from judgment, knowing that our perspective is limited.

May we encourage the efforts of each and be supportive of those who may fall behind.

May we always be aware that the accomplishments of all are enhanced by mutual encouragement and support.

May we be privileged to run our own races well.

May we be glad in our hearts to celebrate the successful completion of all the races in the world.

May our King be pleased with our efforts. Amen.

# Wellsprings

The birth of our forefather Abraham heralded a new era in the world. During a dark time when idol worship permeated the world, Abraham began drawing out God's light, initiating a new awareness of God. It was a time that brought new opportunities for revitalizing the failed mission of Adam, the first man.

Abraham began his life's work by revealing a new path, rejecting the prevalent culture of idolatry. Seeing through the physical barriers that covered the earth, he explored and reopened wellsprings of spiritual understanding obscured by accumulated layers of misunderstanding from the time of Adam. Abraham dug wells and reopened channels that brought him closer to the truth of Torah. Just as water sustains our physical lives, so do the wellsprings of Torah sustain our spiritual lives. Aware of this source of spiritual nourishment, Abraham made it his life's work to open these channels and bring forth an awareness of God.

Our patriarch Isaac saw that the Philistines had blocked the wells of his father, Abraham, in an effort to undo his father's diligent work and to return the world to darkness. Isaac made it his life's work to reopen these channels. His mission was to renew and to continue his father's legacy. Isaac was determined not to let the world revert to the paganism and spiritual deprivation that had preceded his father's great mission. Abraham had brought new understanding to the world and his son Isaac kept the wellsprings of Torah knowledge open and flowing.

Abraham had opened the wells; Isaac had preserved and rededicated them. It was now our patriarch Jacob's life work to draw out the water and to bring new life to the spiritually parched desert that was the world. The idolators again tried to cover over the wells and to prevent the flow of God's wisdom. Jacob removed the obstructions of the idolators and drew out the life-sustaining waters of Torah from its hidden place within the physical world. He spent his life fighting the evil plans of those who sought to continue the blind ways of idolatry and its falsehood. He fought against the evildoers who wanted only for the world to stay in darkness and in ignorance of its true Creator.

Jacob drew out the water of Torah and brought new life to souls. Just as his father and grandfather before him had accomplished their missions, Jacob, too, succeeded in bringing awareness of God and knowledge of Torah into the world. It became the mission of his children, the Children of Israel, to build up the nation whose purpose was to guard the wells and to keep them open, drawing out the spiritual sustenance from its sacred source, the Torah.

In time, and through the diligent efforts of the many generations of Jacob's descendants, the wellsprings of Torah will flow throughout the world, bringing forth a flourishing garden that will cover the earth with God's revelation. In that time all idolatry will be vanquished, and the great mission initiated by Abraham to bring recognition of God into the world will be fully realized.

May it be soon in our days. Amen.

# Wild Horses

From a distance he could see the horses escaping from the barn. As he ran closer and saw that the barn door was wide open, he was dismayed and ashamed because keeping the door locked and the horses securely inside was his responsibility. By the time he reached the barn, only a few horses remained. These were his best-trained horses, and despite the opportunity to escape, they had stayed in their stalls.

Now began the arduous task of finding and gathering in the many horses that had fled. He saddled one of the remaining horses and began searching for the others among the many acres of his family's estate. He knew that once the horses were properly trained and harnessed, they would be productive and diligent workers, but that when not properly directed, they could be destructive and cause much damage. When he found some of the escaped horses, they were trampling the vegetable gardens, scaring the other animals, and trying to knock down the fence surrounding the estate.

One by one, he caught and harnessed each horse. One by one, he took each horse back to the barn and secured it in its stall, making sure when he left that the barn door was locked. In time and through diligent effort, he was able to bring all of the horses under control. Each day he took great care to harness and to train them, accustoming them to following him and obeying his commands.

Their master had learned his lesson. He had been careless and lax in his responsibilities and had not exerted the effort necessary to control and to discipline the horses in his care. His negligence had cost him the time and expense of locating each horse, bringing it back to the barn, and repairing all the damage it had done.

The experience had been a difficult one, and he resolved not to repeat his mistakes. His responsibility as master of the horses was to train them to work diligently and productively. From now on, he would be vigilant in watching over them and exert himself to train them to do their work properly.

In time, the horses became accustomed to their training. Even though it was easier now to keep them under control, their now-wiser master still kept a watchful eye over them and did not let them stray. He knew that even the best trained of his horses were still subject to wild impulses and needed to be supervised. He had become the true master of his horses and lived out his days productively in the service of his King.

# The Apartment

Her Father was the Landlord of a vast complex of apartments. Providing his daughter with a number of keys, He sent her in search of an apartment that was to become her dwelling place. He told her about the different apartments available within the complex, and some of them sounded quite attractive.

She went to the door of an apartment that she was interested in and tried to unlock it, but none of the many keys she had seemed to work. She experimented with turning the knob in different ways and even tried forcing the door open, but no matter how determined she was, the door remained locked.

She tried the door of another apartment. Although not her first choice, she felt that it was a good alternative. Again, she could not find a key that would work. With much effort she turned the knob and tried to get the lock to open, but as with the first, she could not get inside the apartment.

She then went to a third door, and with the first key she tried, the door opened easily. However, when she walked in and looked around, she was disappointed. This apartment was not at all what she had had in mind: The color scheme did not appeal to her and the furnishings were not to her taste. Even though she understood that this apartment was meant for her, she still did not feel comfortable in it. However, despite her initial reaction and discomfort, she realized that this was the apartment that her Father, in His great wisdom, had picked out for her, and thus must be the one most suitable for her.

With that understanding, she opened her heart to her new place and gradually became accustomed to it. As she allowed herself to feel more comfortable, she began to appreciate her new home and to understand its true value. She came to realize that the apartments that she had originally found attractive were actually reflections of the interests and tastes of others. She had been so influenced by their opinions that she had not been following her own true nature and thus had been unable to recognize her true home at first sight.

She was grateful to her Father and thanked Him for not having allowed her to enter apartments that had been attractive to her when she was confused and her vision was limited. She had tried to open doors that were not meant for her. By accepting instead her Father's guidance, she was able to live out her days productively in the dwelling place that was her true home.

May our ears always be open to His teachings.

May our eyes always be open to His presence.

May our hearts always be open to His love. Amen.

# Brothers

Two brothers started out on a car trip and remained together throughout their journey. Great competition existed between the brothers because both had a strong desire to control the car. The older was physically aggressive and had an impulsive nature, and the younger realized that he would never gain control of the car by physically challenging him. He knew that when his older brother was driving, they often went in directions that took them far out of their way, for the older brother's interests and desires were quite different from those of his sibling.

The younger brother, the wiser of the two, was given to study and contemplation. He understood the weaknesses of his older brother. He offered him bribes to relinquish his position at the wheel, knowing that his older brother easily succumbed to various temptations and could be tricked into giving up his driving privilege for a momentary pleasure. The wiser younger brother worked on strategies that gained him access to the steering wheel and maintained his control over the car. He knew, too, that whenever he became distracted, even for a moment, his older brother quickly seized the wheel, never missing an opportunity to regain control of the car.

As the journey progressed, the clever schemes of the younger brother gained him increased driving time and he vigilantly protected his position. He was as persistent and strong willed as his older brother, but used wisdom rather than force to subdue the passions and impulsiveness of his brother. In time, the persistence and patience of the younger brother prevailed, and he was able to bring the aggressive tendencies of his older brother into submission.

The older brother eventually came to accept and to acknowledge the wisdom of his younger brother, understanding that the direction in which his brother was leading them was indeed the best course for both of them. He now willingly allowed his brother to have control of the car. The older brother became a trusting passenger, and the brothers journeyed on together toward their destination.

The brothers had achieved a level of cooperation and mutual understanding, and the competition of their earlier days turned into a journey of common purpose. The older brother understood that when he had been behind the wheel, they had often become lost and found themselves far from their true destination. He came to appreciate his younger brother's understanding and sense of direction. He came to believe in his brother's truth.

When they reached the end of their journey, the brothers parted ways, but they knew that one day they would be reunited to receive recognition for the success of their journey. They would then be linked eternally in harmony and understanding, and the strife of earlier years would be behind them forever.

May it be, with the help of God, that we all find peace and unity, each one with the other.

May it be that all strife be resolved from within and without.

May we soon come together in common purpose and mutual cooperation in the service of our Creator. Amen.

# Brothers, Revisited

Although the brothers were twins, in many ways they were quite different. One was strong and healthy, full of wisdom and energy; the other was weaker, lacking in understanding, and inclined to laziness.

Their Father had sent them off together on an important mission with instructions as to how to accomplish their individual objectives, and had given the stronger brother the responsibility of supporting and caring for his weaker brother. He knew that His weaker son could not function without the assistance of His stronger one, and that His stronger son would be unable to accomplish his important mission without his brother's help and cooperation. The success of their mission was dependent on their ability to work together.

The weaker brother had a self-centered nature and did not appreciate or even acknowledge the importance of his brother's support. He had a strong sense of entitlement and took for granted the support and guidance his brother gave him. The stronger brother repeatedly reminded his brother of their Father's instructions and of the important work that they needed to do, but the weaker brother often turned a deaf ear and continued in his lazy ways and pursuit of pleasure.

The stronger brother worked hard and diligently to follow his Father's directives, persevering despite the resistance of his brother. He encouraged his brother to work harder and not to become distracted, trying to make him understand that he was wasting his time and energy on transitory things. He also pointed out to him the dangers and pitfalls that could impede their progress and affect the success of their mission.

As the years passed, the weaker brother grew in understanding and strength. Over time, he began to see how his pursuit of pleasure left him feeling only momentarily satisfied and did not afford him any lasting benefit. He realized that by following his brother's guidance and example he would feel a real sense of pride and accomplishment. Knowing that he was fulfilling his Father's directives gave him great pleasure and happiness, and he became less self-centered and more appreciative of his brother's help and guidance. By following his brother's ways of truth, he experienced a greater strength of purpose and direction.

Nevertheless, it was still difficult for the weaker brother to overcome his natural tendency to laziness and distraction. He learned to call at such times to his Father for help and to ask his brother for guidance. He began to take pride in the strength of his resolve, and in his ability to overcome the temptations of the moment.

As the weaker brother grew in strength, the stronger brother was able to provide him with even greater levels of guidance and understanding. As they worked together toward their common goal, the two brothers became unified in purpose. Their Father, who knew that their joint mission had presented them with many challenges and difficulties, was pleased with the accomplishments of His sons. Through their mutual persistence and diligence, they had succeeded in their mission. Their journey was now complete.

May we, with God's help, be able to focus our efforts and energies properly and productively.

May we recognize and understand the strength and wisdom of our souls.

May we be able to unite our disparate natures in the true and devoted service of our Creator. Amen.

# The Lost Treasure

At her birth, the King presented his beloved daughter with a beautiful treasure chest filled with precious stones of exquisite colors and shapes. When the young princess was old enough to open the treasure chest, she delighted in looking at the shiny, multicolored gems. Knowing that they were a gift from her Father made her love and value them even more.

She began to notice, however, that each time that she opened her treasure chest, the number of precious stones was fewer. She realized that thieves were stealing its treasure, and although it saddened her greatly, she knew that she had to lock up her beautiful chest and hide it or she would soon be left with nothing. With a heavy heart, she hid what remained of her treasure, but now she no longer had the joy of opening up the beautiful chest to admire the colorful gems. She no longer had access to this precious gift from her Father, but she also knew that she had no alternative. She hoped one day to be able to retrieve her treasure chest from its hiding place and again to gaze at the beautiful stones, but in the meantime, it had to be securely locked and hidden away.

Many years passed, and the princess grew up and moved to a new land where she did not have to be so protective of her possessions. Unlike her birthplace, here there was no threat from thieves. She recalled her beautiful treasure chest and yearned for the pleasure of once again gazing at the jewels inside. To her dismay, however, she could remember neither where she had hidden the chest nor the key. She decided to search for her long-lost treasure. Even though many years had passed, she was determined to seek out and reclaim her beautiful and precious stones.

She journeyed back to the land of her birth and inquired of everyone she met if they remembered her, her family, or her home.

She looked. She searched. She inquired. She wanted to learn as much as she could about the early years of her life. She hoped that revisiting her birthplace might help her to remember where she had hidden the treasure. Her homecoming was a difficult one. She remembered the thieves who had stolen her precious gems, and with sorrow, the reason that she had had to hide them away. However, revisiting her sorrow made her even more determined to find her lost treasure.

During her search, the people that she met were sympathetic and tried in whatever way they could to be helpful. Recognizing the distress of the princess, they hoped that what had been lost to her would be restored. The princess also met a messenger from her Father the King. He explained to her that even though the sympathetic people she had met were trying to be helpful, it was from her Father she needed to ask for help, for only He could provide her with the key to her lost treasure.

It had not occurred to her to ask her Father for help. Although she knew that the treasure had come from Him, and that He had looked after her throughout her life, she had never turned to Him. She understood her mistake, and from then on she called to her Father every day, asking for His guidance, His help, and His understanding. She asked Him to send her teachers to show her the way, and messengers to guide her and to help her to stay on the right path. She assured her Father that she would open her heart to the lessons she needed to learn and the work she needed to do to retrieve her lost treasure. Her determination was single-minded because she greatly yearned for what had been lost to her.

Her Father listened to the heartfelt pleas of His daughter; He, too, was saddened by the loss of her treasure. Knowing well the hearts of His children, He knew that her motives and yearnings were sincere. He sent her signs. He sent her maps. He sent her teachers and messengers to help her in her quest. By calling to her Father, she had received the help that she needed to find her lost treasure chest.

She now studies the maps diligently and listens to her teachers faithfully. Each day she brings renewed determination and devotion to her quest. She knows that her Father's guidance is leading her closer and closer to the lost treasure. She has faith that it is only a matter of time before she realizes her goal and once again has access to her beautiful treasure chest. In the meantime, she pursues her studies and follows the proper path.

She believes that soon she will again be able to gaze at the sparkling gems of her youth, with nothing to fear from the thieves who robbed of her treasure. She works hard each day in pursuit of her lost treasure, and looks forward to the day when a lifetime of yearning and sorrow will end. She hopes not only to recover the hidden treasure chest, but all of the precious stones stolen from her so long ago. She knows that she is following the right path and that her Father is always there to help and to guide her. By continuing in the direction that she has now accustomed herself to traveling, she believes that she will one day find her beautiful treasure chest. She patiently awaits and anticipates that day.

May it come soon. Amen.

# Observations

# Moments

Choices are made at every turn; many are made by default. Without proper preparation, we become bound by habit. Mindful living is the art of life. Openness and receptivity allow us to experience each moment as new. Life can be played like an old tape that keeps repeating itself over and over, a cycle of old formulas no longer relevant. Enslavement can happen when we retain certain behaviors and responses that may have had relevance in the past but have none in the present.

Now is the place to live. The experience of now is precious, a gift to be used and appreciated. Bringing awareness to all that you do will bring understanding in its wake. Prepare yourself to meet your moments. Respect them as the great opportunities they are. Do not sleepwalk through your life, stumbling in the dark and groping for the light.

Keep your eyes open and meet life as it brings gifts and opportunities for growth. Do not run away. Do not hide. Do not be afraid.

Let the Torah be your guide. Let the light of your holy soul lead you. Don't be led by the temptations of pride and arrogance. Be as secure as a child in the arms of a protective father. Don't allow yourself to intimidated, influenced, or coerced by your prideful ambitions and your faulty logic.

Remember who you are and what your mission is. The world is full of illusory traps and you must be careful where you step. Move closer to Torah and to those who teach Torah. Distance yourself from those who are ignorant and who ridicule what they don't understand.

Make your steps purposeful. Use your time wisely. You will

one day be called to task for all your wasted moments. Don't reject your precious gifts: Your Father has given so much. Open your heart in appreciation. Open your heart to Him.

# Opening Channels

I need to take a vacation from me. I need to clear my mind and make myself into an empty vessel, ready to receive. There is so much busyness, so many thoughts, so many concerns. I need to let them go. They interfere with the clear reception of the messages and teachings being continually broadcast from my soul. Our minds create so many disturbances, so much interference, that we become blocked from the great source of wisdom that resides within us all.

All around us are messages. If we truly listened, truly looked and paid attention to the world around us, we could learn so many important lessons. Clearing the channels so that we can receive rather than transmit seems to be contrary to our nature. We approach life actively – talking, doing, and accomplishing our many tasks – but our more receptive nature needs to be developed, too. The art of contemplation has become lost to many of us.

We see ourselves as doers who need to act constantly in order to be. The truth is that we must be before we can act. Do we take good advantage of our time, or just move from one task to the next in a robotic way? Do we perceive the colors in our world? Do we really hear the voices of the people around us? Do we notice their hurt? Do we see their confusion? Do we need to learn to see?

Being awake and aware is the way to open channels. Learning the path of receptivity allows us to live each of our moments mindfully. Tuning in to our inner voice allows us to understand our true direction. How do we live the teachings of the Torah? We can follow a programmed path without proper intent, or we can do each mitzvah with true attention and intention. If we prepare ourselves for our holy work and do it properly, we can cause new sparks of illumination to shine in the world. We have the great opportunity of spending every one of our days bringing new lights of Godliness into our world.

We don't understand our potential, our tremendous ability to change both ourselves and everything around us. Unfortunately, we also have the ability, God forbid, to cause much damage and to bring ourselves and our world into greater darkness. The mindful performance of mitzvot and the careful avoidance of sin transform us and everything around us. Kindness generates kindness. Anger generates anger. Love generates love.

As we go through our days, we often lose our focus. We become involved in our busyness and can't properly evaluate our actions. Have our actions been done truthfully and in God's name, or God forbid, in mindlessness? Every action we do or refrain from doing changes the world. Nothing is trivial.

Mindful living, in keeping with the ways of Torah, will bring greater light into our lives. Being aware at all times of proper service to our Master is our most important work. We must be diligent in this work and receptive to the teachings of our souls. We must take the lessons of Torah into our hearts. We must be vigilant to keep distortions and temptations from lodging in our hearts, creating barriers to proper receptivity.

May we open pathways of proper service of our Master.

May all impediments and obstacles be cleared from our path.

May we always be receptive to the words and teachings of our holy Torah. Amen.

# In the Right Direction

Taking walks among trees and ducks, grass and ponds, brings me back to me. In the course of our days we get involved in our many chores and responsibilities. Although it is important to take care of these responsibilities, they can take us away from our true selves. We get caught up in the accomplishment of our tasks, often losing sight of their underlying purpose. We can become like the builders who saw the boards, nail the crossbeams, and mix the cement, but don't know the purpose of the building they are creating. We focus on the details of what needs to be done, often forgetting why it is being done. We need to stop at some point every day just to catch up with ourselves. Even though we have beepers, mobile telephones, e-mail, and fax machines, and can contact almost anyone anywhere, we are often out of touch with ourselves.

When someone asks you how you are doing, do you really know? If someone asks how your day is going, how will you respond? What criteria will you use to measure or to evaluate if it is going well or not? What is it that needs to go? Where is it that you are going? You travel through each day, but how far have you gone each day? Was it as far as you would have liked? How far would have been adequate?

Each day we need to stop at the side of the road and ask ourselves if we are headed in the right direction. Have we plotted the map of our day, or did we just drive along aimlessly? Were we paying attention to the road and reading the signs along the way, or did we just follow an accustomed course, well traveled but not well thought out? By the end of the day, are we any closer to our destination? Have we even determined what our destination should be? Days can go by quickly, turning into months and years before we even realize the passage of time. When we look back, what are we going to count as our accomplishments? Are we going to look back with pride or with sorrow? Did we make good use of this precious time or did we often spend it mindlessly?

We need to plot our course and to stay on it. We need constantly to evaluate whether we are headed in the right direction, or wasting our time pursuing dead ends or circular roadways. If we see that we have turned away from our prescribed course, we need to correct our mistake and return to the proper road. We must pay attention and give care to preparing each day for that day's journey. At the close of each day we need to evaluate how far we have come and whether we have made good progress. When we are asked how things are going or how we are doing, we should know the answers. If we wait until many years have passed before finding these answers, it may be too late for the changes and the corrections that we all need to make.

Get to know yourself each and every day. Stay in touch with who you are and what your true goals are. Set those goals for yourself and constantly evaluate your progress. One day may not be as productive as another day, but stay on course and try to do better tomorrow. Each day brings new opportunities for progress and development. Don't waste these precious opportunities by not recognizing them, or by failing to take advantage of them.

You must understand your mission. You must learn how best to do your work and how to do it well. Remember why you are doing this work and give it your full attention. Do not leave behind wasted days and misdirected efforts. Do not squander the opportunities of your life, leaving this world with regret and sorrow. Your payment awaits you for a job well done. You must earn it with pride and dedication.

May we all build our fine houses with purpose and understanding.

May our King be pleased with our efforts. Amen.

# Cotton Candy

*Undo the negative habits from the past.*
*Uproot them and replace them with positive habits.*

I waste my time, my energy, my mind, on cotton candy. The taste is quickly gone and there is no satisfaction beyond the momentary, sweet taste. I must involve myself with those things that are sweet but also satisfying beyond the moment.

When we don't plan for and engage in what is beneficial, we run the risk of partaking in what is readily available but of little value. It is easy for us to talk without thinking. It is easy to become absorbed in useless or even, God forbid, negative thoughts when we are not paying attention, when we let our minds wander. When we don't make a conscious effort to focus our minds in valuable directions, we leave the door open for whatever might happen by.

When we become accustomed to the "junk food" of the media and the gossip that surrounds us, we are no longer safeguarding our souls. We are leaving ourselves unprotected from whatever half-thought-out opinions or misguided logic may come our way. We must distance ourselves from the many influences that are ever present and attractive to us when we let down our guard. Keeping away from these attention-getting distractions may seem difficult at first, but with proper attention and planning, new habits can be formed.

Don't let your mind become unoccupied. Don't let your thoughts wander: Bring them back. Always be ready with positive and important material with which to occupy yourself. Don't wait until the moment of distraction arises. Prepare in advance.

When you are hungry, don't reach for "fast food," which may provide momentary relief from your hunger, but will not digest well or provide much nutritional benefit. Keep your pantry well stocked. Prepare your diet in advance. Don't reach for whatever is convenient and easily accessible. When you need nourishment, provide yourself with satisfying and nutritious food that will give you strength and endurance. Plan your diet. Properly prepare and cook your meals, even your snacks. Eat slowly and digest well. Let what you ingest strengthen you and satisfy your hunger.

Discriminate. Choose consciously rather than accept passively. Let all your actions come through conscious attention. Be awake and stay alert. What seems harmless may be misleading and dangerous influences derived from unholy sources. Be watchful and on your guard. You came here in a clean and pure state. Protect yourself from the ever-present dirt and grime that surrounds you. Be careful. Don't let yourself be fooled. Cotton candy tastes sweet for a moment, but the taste quickly fades and leaves you empty and craving more.

Eat well. Be well nourished. Be satisfied and grow strong as you reach toward your goals with purpose and direction. Amen.

# Hurt, Pain and Anger

Perfection is the way of God. Striving for perfection is the true way of human beings but we become confused, we lose our way. We look for short-term solutions to problems that require long-term efforts. We hurt each other with our anger. We are angry because we feel hurt and then want to hurt others in return.

Anger is a poison. It makes us ill and causes pain and misunderstanding. Losing ourselves in anger is egocentric: We become focused on our own pain and rage. We become blind to others and we lose sight of ourselves. In our anger we forget God, we forget our work, we lose touch with our souls.

We have been hurt, oppressed, and abused, and in our pain, we want to strike back. We may victimize others or victimize ourselves. We don't know what to do with these tremendous feelings of disrespect and insult.

Why do others so disregard my feelings?
Why aren't they concerned with my feelings?
Can't they see the pain they inflict?
Are they so hurt themselves that they are numb to the pain they
     inflict on others?
Can't their hearts feel a connection to the pain in the hearts of
     their victims?
Have their own hearts become blocked, unaware, and insensitive
     to the feelings of anyone but themselves?
Do they even know their own feelings, or are their hearts blocked
     off even from themselves?

Hurt and pain form a cycle. When we are caught up in this cycle, we lose touch with our true identity. We forget our royal origins. We forget our Father the King. In moments of clarity, we may come to understand our self-destructive behavior, to have glimpses of regret and shame. But then we return to old, ingrained habits and continue on the familiar and destructive path that we have set for ourselves, one that takes us further and further from our true selves.

We make wrong turns, but instead of turning around and correcting our mistakes, we persist in following incorrect paths that lead us far from those we were meant to travel. When we find ourselves unsure and straying, we must acknowledge our wrong turns and make every effort to return to our proper path. This course requires vigilance. We must be aware and on our guard, because old habits will return as soon as we start to become distracted.

Anger leads to regret. You can ignore your shame and continue in your angry ways, or you can use it to bring you back in true repentance to your Father. If you excuse and rationalize your anger rather than admitting your mistake, you will become accustomed to your angry behavior, and it will become an ingrained response. Ingrained behavior is difficult to uproot and makes returning to your proper path only more difficult.

Start today to take responsibility for your mistakes: I have sinned, dear God; please forgive me. Please help me see and follow the proper path. Help me forgive myself so that I may develop the confidence to fight the stubborn behaviors rooted in the past. Help me at all times to be vigilant and careful not to stray from my true direction in life. Let my eyes be open to the dangers, temptations, and pitfalls that I may encounter at any time. Let me understand and be mindful of my choices and recognize dangers when they present themselves. Make me so aware at all times of Your Presence, dear God, that I will be ashamed to wander from Your path.

I need Your help.

I need Your support.

I need Your direction.

I need Your guidance.

I need Your strength to help me rectify the mistakes of the past, and to guard me from potential dangers in the present. Let me walk in Your ways, dear God. Open my ears to Your teachings. Let me free myself of sin so that I may do Your work properly. Keep me from shame, keep me from regret, and let me walk in pride in Your ways, now and forever. Amen.

# Our Inner Teacher

We play follow-the-leader. We do what others do, thinking that it must be acceptable. Could so many others be misdirected? Surely there is safety in numbers? Yet the only truly safe number is one.

Following the paths of others leads us astray; following the ways of others can take us far from our own true paths. The people we come in contact with may be misguided, or they may indeed be following correct paths – but paths specific to them and not appropriate for us. We need to connect with our inner teacher. Just as each individual's genetic code is unique, so each person's mission is individual and to be accomplished only by him or her. When we don't pay attention to our inner guides, we imitate what we see around us. We want to fit in, to be accepted and acceptable. By letting ourselves be influenced by our environment, we become diverted from our true purpose, chameleons blending in with our surroundings.

Ask yourself: What is my work? What course is appropriate for me to follow? Our true direction never lies in simply mirroring what we see around us. Others may be following one another in the way of a herd, staying together for reasons of mutual convenience or security that are not in the best interests of each individual. Although it is true that we need to connect to other people, we must do so without being absorbed by these relationships. In our connection to others, we must be both a part of the community and apart from it. A delicate balance exists between the roles we play within our community and in the accomplishment of our specific missions.

Teachers who lead and direct others must do so with the utmost respect and sensitivity for the uniqueness and specific abilities of each student. Teaching should never resemble an assembly line. Each soldier in God's army has a special and important position. It may seem that the responsibilities of an officer are of greater importance than those of a common soldier. Yet the contribution of each, when the job is done well and to the best of one's ability, is equally precious in the eyes of the Commander-in-Chief.

Our first task is to determine our place in this great army. We need to discern our specific missions, and then to perform them with love and determination. Our work is ours alone, and we must search within ourselves to understand what that work is before we can do it properly. Don't avoid this search by mindlessly following the herd. Listen to your inner guide and follow your unique and precious path in truth. Take the opportunities you have been given and make the most of them. That, my friend, is why you are here.

# Marching Under the Banner of God

Why do we feel the need to control and to manipulate others?
Why do we feel the need to control and to manipulate our environment?
What restlessness is there within us that seeks to make the world conform to the selfish interests of the ego?

A primary lesson in soulful living is acceptance. How do I know that my understanding is superior to someone else's? Even if I think it is, perhaps he or she is not now able or willing to hear my words. Will imposing my understanding be helpful or could it, God forbid, cause harm? When I am asked for my opinion or advice, do I respond based on my own ego-understanding, or on the other person's true needs? My friend is on a different journey, and may be at a different point in his or her journey than I am in mine. Do I speak with arrogance and superiority, or with love and understanding? Do I know better than my friend?

Do we need to make everyone conform to one way of being in the world?
Do we have to feel threatened by what is different?
If I love another, can I help him or her without intruding and imposing my own ideas and agendas?
Is it ever possible to heal the world through force?
Can we ever transform the world by imposing our will?

The will of God underlies everything. Our job is to understand His will and follow it, not to try to change the world, which with our limited understanding and narrow perspective can only cause damage. To search out and to reveal the truth of God's will is our work. When we follow our own flawed understanding, we only pervert this truth. We need to dig and to search; revealing the truth is a time-consuming and arduous task. We must refrain from hasty judgments and look inward, not outward. Our influence in the world will be felt only over time, and only through the vehicle of love.

Force or violence has never endeared anyone to anyone or anything. We can intimidate others into doing many things, but never into having true love and respect for us. If you seek truly to influence one individual or the entire world, first align yourself with the Will of the Holy One Blessed be He. The weakness of the individual ego causes it to rely on intimidation. When we follow the path of God, we gain tremendous strength and authority that are far beyond normal human limitations.

Search within, not outside of yourself, and strengthen your connection with God, the Source of all. Instead of trying to change all that you see around you, turn inward to learn from your own source of wisdom. Look to your Creator for help and guidance; look into His Torah to show you the way.

If you truly want to change the world, all is within your reach, but you must change the world only according to His plan and only with love. The power of a person who follows the ways of the Creator is great; the power of anyone who follows his or her ego is weak and limited.

Become a peaceful warrior in the great legion of your Commander. Come under His banner and follow His commands. In joining God's forces you will vanquish your enemies from within and without. The solitary soldier with a personal banner eventually falls in battle. Marching under the banner of the Torah legions, you will be victorious.

# Traveling on our True Paths

How do we become so lost?

How do we become so stuck in our ways?

How do we turn into our own enemies?

How do we become so insensitive to ourselves as well as to others?

How do we cause pain to others, often without even realizing it?

How do our hearts become so filled with pride and self-importance?

How do we injure ourselves time and time again, yet pay no attention to the pain?

How do we start out from the grand station of existence only to become derailed, so far off the tracks?

At every turn we make decisions; at every turn we are given opportunities. Each stop we make takes us either closer to our destination or farther from it. With each act, each word, each step, we bring ourselves either closer to the accomplishment of our missions or farther from their achievement. As we travel along our paths, we are challenged time and time again. The people we meet and the situations we find ourselves in either help us accomplish our missions or distance us from the work that we are on earth to do. We need to focus on our destination, on the true road that will take us there, even though we don't know exactly where we are headed. Our inner guide, like a compass, will point us in the proper direction, but it is up to us to follow in the direction that the arrow indicates.

Step by step, moment by moment, we travel our paths. Unless we consult our inner compass, we go unprepared and unthinking into our futures. When we stop to assess our position, we may find that we have gone entirely out of our way. Perhaps with only a slight change of course we will be back on the proper path, but first we must stop, evaluate our progress, and check our position. The more often we do so, the better able we will be to go forward. If we stop only occasionally, we may find that we have lost time and effort pursuing dead ends.

Chart your progress. Check your position – but only in relation to yourself, not to others. Your mission is yours alone. The abilities you have been given are unique to you. The challenges you have been given are specific to your particular mission. At a given point on the path, you might be achieving your best effort while someone else is lagging behind. Your life path is yours alone. Your accomplishments will be judged according to a measuring stick individual to you. Don't look to others to determine your success. No two courses are run the same. Yours may be a solitary journey traveling on side streets and through quiet neighborhoods; others may be following a more public route through large, populated centers. Do not compare your path with the paths of others. Follow your own itinerary and be faithful to it.

Pray that you do not become stuck in dead ends. Pray that you may live your life in accordance with your inner wisdom, which will guide you and lead you toward the successful accomplishment of your mission. Find your inner compass and follow your true direction. Follow faithfully the lessons that your Father has given you in His Torah. Your work is important and it is yours alone. Do it well!

# Paying Attention

Welcome this time – a time of change, a time of newness. Clear out old, outdated thoughts. Meet this new time with open eyes and an open heart. Empty your mind of the many thoughts constantly coming in. Simplify the busyness of your life. Look at your surroundings with the wonder of a child, observing everything with curiosity and a thirst to learn. The textures of tree bark, birds flapping wings in flight – look as if you have never looked at them before. Delight in the many sights and sounds of life unfolding. Use your gift of understanding to unravel its many secrets. Learn the many lessons that life comes to teach. Be a student of your world and connect your being to the wisdom of God's countless creations.

This world is a place for learning and growing. You can blossom like a flower, stretching your petals toward the sky. You can feel the movement of the wind, and watch as dry leaves tumble along their way. You have been like a machine running mechanically and blindly, unaware of the beauty and diversity of the life that surrounds you. Follow the bird in flight. Smell the fragrance of the moist earth. Watch ripples as they play on the surface of the water. Stay still and observe in silence. Refrain from the inclination to speak, to touch, to move. Sit and listen, receive and absorb the lessons of awareness and peace.

A time of calm. A time of receptivity. A time of reflection. What color is the sky? Look at the balance of light and shadow. Observe the goose's silhouette against the shimmering waters that surround her. Look up and look down, right and left. Each time you look, you will see something new. Pay attention to your ever-changing world. Be still in your place as a student of the world. Learn the lessons of deliberation and thoughtfulness. Observe how colors change over time. Notice the faces of those around you. Control the many busy thoughts that intrude on your reflection. Push them gently away as you gaze with childlike attention at the design in a fabric or the shininess of metal.

You have formed many opinions. You have made many decisions. You watch the clock and move swiftly through each day. Where did this day go? Was I mindful of what was said to me? Did I even hear it? Did I pay attention? Was I alert today, or did the day pass by without my even noticing? Did I experience this day's time, or did it just go without my being aware of its passing?

Don't lose yourself in time. Don't lose time to unthinking and routine behavior. Wake up and stay alert! These moments are your opportunities. Understand the preciousness of each moment and open yourself up to the many lessons that each new day brings. Be able to remember your moments as filled with attention, purpose, and dedication rather than with regret at the passage of time. Look back and remember the time you spent in observation and understanding.

Make use of your mind and control its content. Guard the doors of your soul and direct your thoughts properly. This day will go by quickly: Don't let it leave empty and unfilled. Your Creator has given you the gift of the precious moments of this precious day. Receive this gift with appreciation. Fill this day with love and be grateful for each moment of your life.

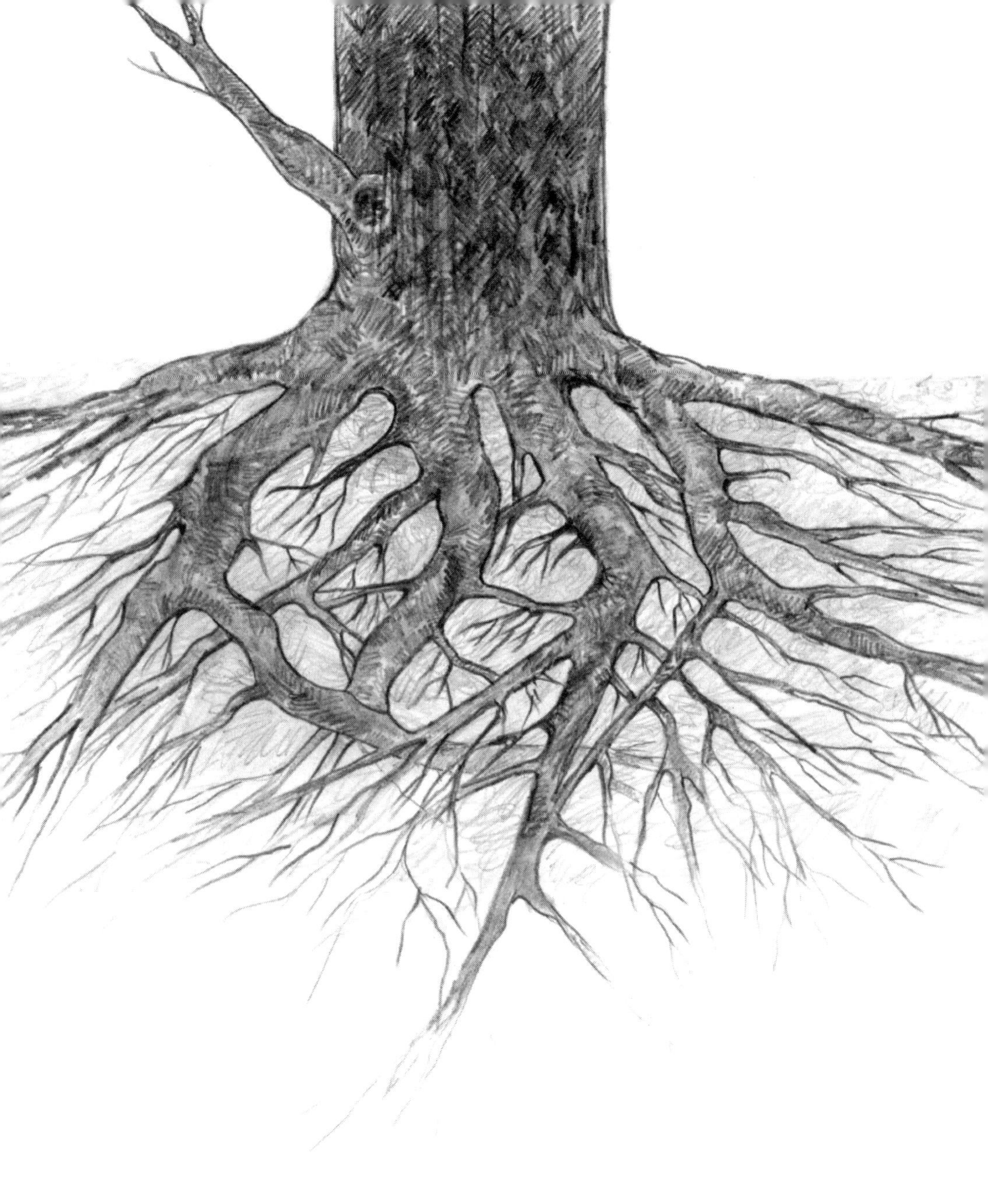

# Meditations

# Shabbat

Shabbat is my healing time.
Shabbat gives me strength.
Shabbat is my oasis, my respite.
I draw sustenance from God's gift.
I feel secure in His light.
Anxieties leave me, and I feel His protection.
Please let me feel Your light, O God.
Please surround and guard me with Your heavenly light.
Please let me sit here mindfully in Your presence, attached and
    connected to You.
My small flame yearns to return to the Source of warmth and
    light.
Let my flame be my guide.
Let my flame lead me closer to You.
Let my flame be absorbed into Your great and holy light.
O Lord, please don't desert me.

# Clearing the Land

King David spent his life in battle, freeing the land of Israel of the foreign elements preventing the construction of the Holy Temple and the establishment of a permanent monarchy. Everywhere King David turned, he was faced with elements whose purpose was to block a greater manifestation of God's presence in the world. The battle was – and is – between the forces that promote awareness of God in the world and the forces that would have the world remain in darkness. This battle, fought over and over throughout the generations, is a battle that also takes place in our hearts. To establish a permanent home for the Divine Presence takes work and great effort, and we must never stop fighting.

Pockets of idolatry, abuse, and degradation littered the Holy Land. Other lands had such filth in their midst, but in the Holy Land of Israel, even small areas of defilement and desecration could not be tolerated. They needed to be rooted out and obliterated. No remnants of the abominations of the evildoers could remain.

King David spent his life locating and destroying all traces of evil within the land. He knew that the Divine Presence could not dwell in a land that harbored desecrators of Torah and tolerated evil within its borders. The battles were relentless; there was no rest from this work. Freeing the land of its nests of predators and leeches was an all-consuming effort. To secure and prepare the land to receive God's presence was the most important of missions. King David worked tirelessly to rid it of the impediments that kept the Great House of Israel from being established.

A holy land must be emptied of sin before its King can come. A holy soul must likewise rid itself of sin before it can receive the Godly presence. Just as King David fought to reclaim those parts of the land to which idolators had laid claim, so too must we rid ourselves of the negative elements within us that estrange us from our King. He yearns to be invited into our lives, but He cannot enter places of uncleanliness, and as long as we retain these pockets within, we will remain estranged from Him.

Let us reclaim our souls from the elements of sin that have established a presence within us. Just as we seek to free our Holy Land to receive the great and Holy Temple, so too let us free our holy souls to be able to connect with the great and Holy Source of all existence.

May we, like King David, work tirelessly toward this goal.

May we stay focused in our efforts.

May we soon free our land and be able to welcome the return of our King. Amen.

# Illumination

Peace fills places where dirt has been removed; empty, tranquil spaces replace pockets of bitterness and resentment. Into these new spaces love and care can now flow. Impurity for so long inhibited the flow of peace in the house and interfered with the transfer of holy light within the house. Places of darkness obstructed the light from shining forth. Animating and invigorating light was withheld, and the house was unable to receive the flow of holy energy.

Bit by bit, the blocked areas are being cleared away. Channels are being opened and the house can now receive a greater flow of light. The process has been long and painstaking. Much dirt had accumulated over time, forming layers that became barriers. Removing the prodigious accumulation was a time-consuming effort; keeping the areas clear is an ongoing task.

We must be vigilant and alert to the particles of impurity anxious to dwell in our houses. Once an area has been secured, we must be on guard to keep new particles from forming blockages. But our efforts bring great reward. A house open to the flow of precious light into its structure receives life-giving energy. This animating light of peace provides awareness and clarity. The clear spaces are able to hold and to emit the holy light shining through them.

A house with an accumulation of dirt and grime dims the light and causes a darkness within. When these pockets of uncleanliness are cleared away, the transformed house glows with an inner illumination that makes other houses look dull by comparison. Other homeowners, inspired by the beauty of such a house, will follow the ways of its owner. Experiencing the emanation of holy light and naturally drawn to it, they will begin renovating their own homes, dismayed that they had allowed them to become so blocked up and dirty. An illuminated house stands as an example and a model for all the houses in a community.

Let us open the doors and windows of our houses and allow the holy light to shine forth, unobstructed.

Let us commit ourselves to keeping the channels open and flowing.

May we soon see a proliferation of brightly illuminated houses within all the communities of the world. Amen.

# Learning to Swim

I want to learn to swim, to glide through the water, moving with purpose and direction. Free of the earth's gravitational pull, I want to move with grace, stroking my way into the future. I want to learn the secret ways of the sea creatures that swim swiftly and freely below the water's surface.

The sea is not our natural environment. Human beings need firm earth and clear air. They sail the seas, fish in them, and drink from them, but need to return and reconnect with the earth from which they were formed. To learn the ways of the sea is to explore the hidden source of all life. To navigate the waters connects us to that hidden part of ourselves that we yearn for but understand least.

We know we are not only earthly beings, that we have an importance beyond our physicality, but we stand on the shore-line afraid to explore, to investigate the secrets that lie hidden from our view within the great sea. We are drawn to the water but stand rooted on the shore.

I want to explore and to navigate the seas. I yearn to feel the refreshing water surrounding and supporting me as I move myself along in new directions toward my destination. I want to feel comfortable within the life-sustaining sea, to know the ways of these life-giving waters and accustom myself to them. I have been earthbound for so long. I need to feel the freedom of traveling the seas, its cool waves carrying me further along in the journey.

May I be granted the ability to navigate these precious waters. May I move purposefully and productively toward my destination. May I be able to understand and to appreciate the great significance of my journey. Amen.

# White Geese

A different perspective: interspersed among the brown and black geese are white ones. They stand out among their peers. When they lift their necks, they look dignified and royal. The orange of their beaks matches the orange of their webbed feet, which adapt to both land and water. Creatures comfortable in both elements, where is their true place? Which environment is their true home? I like to watch them swim effortlessly through the water, but they seem equally comfortable walking on the earth.

I have not been as comfortable walking on this earth. I have tripped and stumbled many times. The earth has been filled with obstacles and impediments; some I have been able to navigate, others took me my surprise. I have been bruised and hurt by this earth; it has inflicted many wounds. I have often fallen and, bleeding and scared, picked myself up, cleaned myself off as best I could, and continued on my journey. Unlike the geese, I could find no solace floating on the comforting waters: I had not learned to swim. All environments seemed dangerous to me.

A goose walks and swims by instinct, but if it has been hurt, all environments become hazardous. Geese instinctively do what is beneficial for their survival, as do healthy human beings. If a goose's wings become damaged, it cannot fly; if its feet become damaged, it cannot walk. A goose taken out of its habitat may develop maladaptive behavior, and a gosling taken from its mother will become lost and disoriented.

The dual nature of human beings is represented by the letter, *aleph*. The *aleph* is the first letter of the word *ish* (man), and the first letter of the name of the first man, Adam. The diagonal line running through the aleph represents the split of human nature.

To the left of the diagonal is the leg with which we walk the earth. To the right of the diagonal is the hand with which we reach toward the heavens.

The higher instincts of human beings come from their higher soul, the *neshama*; the baser instincts come from their animal soul, the *nefesh*. Like geese, we can navigate both environments; unlike geese, we are not always able to do so harmoniously. We are drawn to the earth but feel pulled toward the water. We often spend our lives in conflict, going first in one direction then in another. Human beings can, however, join these two aspects to function in harmony. The leg of the aleph can serve the hand of the aleph. We can both walk the earth and swim the seas. We can use the nefesh as a vehicle to carry the neshama to higher places.

Geese also have wings. If we learn to walk the earth and swim the seas, we will fly above them both. We must learn to walk mindfully and to swim soulfully. We will then transcend the limitations of both and to bring ourselves closer to the heavens.

May we walk with care on the earth.

May we swim productively toward our goals.

May we learn the secret of flying heavenward. Amen.

# Flying Lessons

I see the goose soaring, spreading its wings, gliding through the air. It seems effortless and natural. What is the natural way of human beings? We don't have wings, yet we are capable of flight. What keeps us earthbound? Misunderstanding? Confusion? Fear?

We must first acknowledge the existence of our wings and know that we have the capacity to fly. Once we come to that understanding, we must have flying lessons, and devote time, effort, and energy to learning the skills of flying. We need to practice flapping our wings as we train ourselves to leave the ground.

We must look toward the sky and reach toward the stars. Despite our earthly attachment, we must acknowledge and recognize our ability to take flight. We must believe in our ability to fly, and strive with mind and heart to learn the important lessons of flight. We may, God forbid, spend all our days rooted to the earth. We may look down at our feet and limit ourselves to walking the earth. In doing so, however, we will be ignoring the spirit within us that longs to spread its wings, to soar above the earth.

Am I a dreamer? Do I dream of things that are not possible, or that are beyond the limitations of our human capabilities? No. We were born to fly as surely as any bird. The potential that lies within us is waiting to be discovered, waiting for our bodies to awaken from the slumber of their earthly sleep. Our souls cry out to us, but often we don't hear them. Our senses have become dulled to our voices within. We are not listening. We pay no attention.

We must open our ears. We must open our eyes. We must open our minds and our hearts to the voices of our souls. The secret of flying resides within us. The wisdom is there to be discovered. The lessons are there waiting to be learned. We must open the channels and awaken from our earthly sleep. We must become alert and receptive to the still, small voice crying out to be heard. But first of all, we must believe that we are creatures of the skies, that we have wings. We must long to stretch out our beautiful wings and let the wind carry us to greater heights.

Do not be afraid: leave your confusion behind. You were made to fly, but you have forgotten your true nature and have attached yourself to the earth. Free yourself of earth's gravity, and follow the voice within. It is time, my friend. Take my hand and let us learn to fly together. Come with me on this great journey as we leave the ground and venture above the trees and mountains toward the open blue sky. Don't delay. Each moment is precious, and our Father yearns to welcome us as we travel higher and closer to our true destination – the presence of our Father, the presence of our King.

# Toward Freedom

Please help me, dear God, rid myself of negative thoughts.

Help me, dear God, detach from the pain of the past.

Help me let go of the trauma and the hurt still residing in my heart.

Help me move forward in love, in joy, and in Your service.

Help me leave the oppression of my youth behind and go forward in freedom.

I need Your help, dear God.

I need Your love and support.

I need to feel the light of Your presence as I make my way out of the darkness.

Please extend Your hand so that I may climb out of the pit.

I stumble as I try to climb and need Your help to strengthen my footsteps.

I am trying to move toward the light, but I falter at times and become stuck in my sorrow.

I need Your guidance to help me move forward in my climb.

I am weak and inclined to stop, but knowing You are there to support me gives me the courage and the strength to continue.

Even though in moments of despair I have turned away from You, You have never abandoned me.

Whenever I have been lost, You have kept me from harm.

Please, my Lord, bring me into the light of Your presence.

Please, my Savior, keep me from the elements of darkness that would come to envelop me.

Please, my God, keep me from harm as I make my way unsteadily onto Your path: the path of true and wholehearted service, the path of righteousness. Amen.

# Lessons

# The Tapestry

*Days of purpose, days of fulfillment*

I have a specific job to do, but I must search within and without for the work that is best suited to me. I must come to know my strengths and my areas of greatest challenge, matching the abilities that God gave to me with the opportunities that He has provided. I must not waste time or any of the precious resources I have been given. Everything is a gift.

Will I use this gift well? Will I, with God's help, transform my opportunities and my challenges into something beneficial and productive? Will I match my abilities to the work that I am best suited to do? Will I overcome the obstacles that I find along the way and recognize these obstacles before I trip over them?

I walk carefully but with alacrity. Time is a valuable resource that must be understood and appreciated. Time is a gift from my Master: I must not squander this gift. When I am called on to give an accounting, will I feel shame at the blank spaces when idleness and distraction overcame me? I appreciate the gift of each moment, and keep in mind always the Source of this gift.

My work is my mission: It is what I am most suited to do. I pray every day to be able to receive and to understand my instructions. Each day I am assigned a specific workload. What I don't accomplish today may never get done if I procrastinate, or may take an inordinate amount of time to do later on.

We are provided each day with the opportunities and circumstances needed for that day's work. We have to recognize and to understand what must be done, and do it expeditiously and with dedication. We must remember Who sends us our assignments and that we are in the service of the King.

At the end of each day, evaluate the day's progress and determine where you fell short of your goals. Learn from your mistakes and resolve to do better tomorrow, thus avoiding the shame of repeated mistakes, unevaluated and uncorrected. Use your time and your talents wisely. Appreciate your gifts and use them well. This day will not come again. Today's opportunities will not be here tomorrow: Seize them so they don't pass you by.

Each day is a thread that makes up the tapestry of your life: Create a tapestry that is whole and complete. Each thread contributes its own color and texture to the work of your life. Do not leave this work unfinished. You will be called to task for your incomplete assignments and will feel shame for your empty days and lack of effort. The rewards of your work are great, but you must earn them. Strive for excellence and put forth your best effort. Your days will go by quickly. Avoid the sorrow of looking back at your days with regret and sorrow, knowing that your mission remained incomplete and your time was spent unwisely.

Be able instead to rejoice in your accomplishments with the acceptance and approval of your Father the King. Offer Him your finest fruits, those obtained with your best efforts and toil. Do not be lazy or lax in your work; your remuneration will be commensurate with your efforts and you could, God forbid, be left with empty hands and a sorrowful heart.

At the end of our days, may we be able to look back with pride, not regret.

May our Father find that our efforts have met the standards He has set for us.

May we merit offering to our Father full and productive days spent in His service. Amen.

# Sickness and Health

Give your love. Find your passion and let it flow. Draw your deepest feelings up from your inner well. The soul within you longs to be heard. Give her your attention. Allow her to find expression in your heart and understanding in your mind. Your soul yearns to attach itself to holiness. She cries out for the nourishment of Torah and mitzvot, longing to be closer to her Heavenly Source.

We don't pay attention to our souls; we are too busy. The busyness of our lives distracts us, deafening us to our inner voice. We have things that need to be done, matters to attend to. We can't linger in our prayers or take time away from what we consider the necessities of life, and so our souls suffer in their abandonment.

The flame within us is imprisoned by the materialism of our lives. Alienated and ignored, our souls cannot warm us or generate their heat. Without the radiance of our souls, we become susceptible to the many temptations and infectious diseases that plague humankind. These diseases are ever ready to attack and to take hold at the slightest opportunity. We must strengthen the flame within and guard the precious generator of our existence.

Our souls are the sources of our lives. They keep our bodies functioning and supply us with the spiritual essence that distinguishes us from all other life. Because of our souls, we connect to Godliness and are aligned to the spiritual splendor of our Creator. When we pay attention to our souls and allow them to illuminate us, we can raise ourselves to levels inaccessible even to angels. Our potential is great, yet we often neglect the inner powerful light.

The expression of our spiritual beings restores the proper order of existence. It is our glorious souls who should rule over us, not our earthly bodies. By allowing our physical side to rule, we diminish that part of ourselves that is divine. We raise up the mundane over the holy. We become like the other earthly forms of life around us when we trade our precious birthright for the pleasures of our next meal. We give precedence to what is temporary instead of what is eternal. We forget about the greatness of our souls and allow the temptations of our worldly existence to exert their influence over us.

Wake up your sleeping mind – it is not doing its job. Instead of guarding the gates of your soul, it dozes while diseases infiltrate her, unnoticed. They have found a home within and brought darkness to reside in your heart.

Our souls cry out for us to wake up and guard our posts, but we have been lulled into a dreamlike state and pay no attention. We have become accustomed to our illness; it even seems natural to us for our souls to suffer in their abandonment.

The cure is in your hands. The illness can be healed. As long as your soul resides within you, it is never too late. The prescription for health is sincere and heartfelt repentance. Wake up to your wrong-doings. Drive away the infectious diseases that have laid siege to your soul. Fight for your health with determination and resolve. It is a battle you can win, but you must ask your Heavenly Father for help, love and support. Beseech Him to open up your heart to healing. Open your mind to His Torah, and keep a close guard against the foreign elements of disease. Learn from your mistakes, and resolve to avoid them in the future. This work will take your best efforts, your energy, and your dedication, but no work is of greater importance.

Allow the healing wellsprings of Torah to envelop you. Let them purify you and rid you of disease and impurity. Let the inner light of your soul take its rightful place as master over your physical inclinations. Let your soul be your crowning glory.

May all our souls shine forth, reflecting the great and enduring light of our Creator, our Lord, Blessed be He. Amen.

# From Love and With Love

To serve with love. To serve for love. To act with love. To act for love. The root of your prayer, the root of your actions, the root of all you do and all you are must be love. You must love your God. You must love His creations. You must love yourself.

The concept of self-love seems egocentric. Aren't we supposed to be selfless? Yet if we are unable to love ourselves, we will also be unable truly to love others. To our Creator, we are beloved. He loves the work of His hands, and has bestowed goodness on His creations. As recipients of the goodness of our God, we must understand our inherent value. Since the Master of the Universe has bestowed life upon us, by virtue of that gift, we must know our worth. The Hand that formed us created the highest mountain and all that dwells in the depths of the sea. Each of us has a unique place within creation and a unique mission. What each of us brings to the world cannot be brought by anyone else.

If we can each realize the potential that we have been given, with God's help we can change the world, bringing it and ourselves closer to God. The task is awesome. The responsibility is great. We must know our worth and take our places among those who wholeheartedly serve their Master, withstanding whatever resistances or obstacles that come our way. We may be ridiculed, we may even be scorned or insulted, but we are strengthened by knowing that we are soldiers in God's army. Whatever battles we need to fight, we must fight, but from love and with love.

When Phinehas drew his sword, it was drawn with love for God and for the love of his people. His was not an act of hatred or revenge, but of love befitting a descendant of Aaron, the high priest. Phinehas knew his worth. He knew that he had to put a halt to evil to restore the good. Had he been lacking in confidence in his value as a soldier serving in God's army, he would not have been able to act. With complete trust in God and in the capabilities that had been given to him by God, Phinehas was able to act and to bring about a great sanctification of God's name.

Few of us will ever have the opportunity of acting in such a public and dramatic manner to sanctify God's name, but we are all given many opportunities each day to do our own works of sanctification. Know your value – it is your strength. Remember who your Master is, and to Whom you are responsible. Serve Him with love. Act with purity in your service.

May your motivation be like that of Phinehas, may his memory be for a blessing, pure and unwavering. May you have complete faith and trust in your Creator. May all your actions be done with love and with a whole heart. Amen.

# Your True Identity

Separation. To move away. To look from a distance. When you are in the middle of all the busyness that surrounds you, you become part of that busyness. You cannot discern where you end and others begin. You become integrated with and attached to all the busyness of life around you. You must disengage.

Who are you? How do you differentiate between yourself and others? If you venture an opinion, is it yours? If you have a thought, do you know its origin? What belongs to you, your life, your family, your work? We identify ourselves with many labels. Others may see us in terms of the different roles we take on in our work, in our relationships, and in our community. But who are we? If we were to leave our homes, families, and work and travel to a foreign land where no one knew us and the customs were unfamiliar to us, who would we be then? How would we be able to identify ourselves? How would others identify us? Who would we be when separated from all that is familiar to us?

We all come into this world as strangers. During the course of our lives we come to see ourselves first as children and then as parents, teachers, businesspeople, athletes, or artists; as community-minded or as involved in more personal pursuits. We become a part of the times in which we live. We are affected either positively or, God forbid, negatively by the social customs and structures in our environment. If we were to separate ourselves from all the people, places, and objects that define our lives, who would we be then?

We are like actors who have been put into particular roles. Over time, the stage setting changes, the costumes change, the time period changes, and within these parameters we play our parts. We share our stage with other actors who play their specific roles. The script indicates the story line to be followed and the situations that each actor will face in any given scene. You have been given your role, and it is up to you to give your performance. What will you bring to your part? Within the parameters that have been set up for you, how well will you perform?

The stage you are on contains many different influences. Which of these influences will you follow? Which ones will you reject? When you are faced with different circumstances, which guidelines will you follow, in which direction will you go? Will you follow the guidelines of your teachers? The advice of your parents? The ways of your friends? Will you follow the majority opinion, or that of the minority? On what basis will you decide? How will you determine your proper direction given the many – and often conflicting – influences around you?

You must separate yourself. Leave all the noise and distraction and find a quiet place to know yourself. Out in the busy marketplace, you can easily become lost. You hear so many voices that it is easy to become confused. Listen to the inner voice of your soul, the essential you, the actor freed from his or her role. Wherever you find yourself, wherever you go, the soul within you is uninfluenced by the world's distractions. Your soul is your source of truth, a truth that does not and will not change, a truth that is not dependent on outside circumstances. Your soul is your true identity: Discover who you are by searching for that unique part of yourself that can lead you on your proper path.

Your inner voice can help you distinguish between the truth and the falsehood around you, and lead you on a path toward what will enrich you; it can also protect you from what can mislead or confuse you. Your inner voice speaks quietly and cannot be heard over the noise of the world. Move away from the noise and find a time and a place of quiet, an undisturbed sanctuary. Become acquainted with your most essential self by spending time with your soul and giving her your attention. Your soul will guide you and help you see clearly and truthfully. Your soul will help you understand Torah and warn you of improper influences.

Your soul will help you connect yourself to God, and direct you toward your proper path. Give her your ear by paying attention, by choosing not to be distracted. Appreciate and value the direction of your inner guide.

No matter where you travel, no matter in what circumstances you find yourself, your soul remains constant and unchanging, your true identity and the truth of your existence. Let your soul be your teacher: Follow the direction of your higher self. Come to know who you truly are and you will come to know what you are here to do.

Please help us open our ears to your truth, dear God.

Please help us understand and follow the path of your truth.

May our days be filled and fulfilled in the service of your truth. Amen.

# Your Holy Presence

Sitting in Your house, I feel safe. Acknowledging Your presence strengthens me with feelings of security and peace. I know that You, my God, watch over me, that You love and care for the work of Your hands. The roots of our fears are misperception and misunderstanding: The world is full of the glory of Your presence. The difficulties of our lives derive from our lack of awareness of Your presence. What we see with our eyes distracts us from true seeing. What we hear with ears distracts us from true hearing. When our senses are engaged, we cannot see or hear Your presence.

Our minds are a constant stream of thoughts, our hearts a constant stream of desires. When we do not consciously focus on You and on Godly living, we are led by our senses to confusion, fear, and too often, despair. When we pray, meditate and study Torah, we allow the awareness of Your presence to fill our minds and to enter our hearts. We must make the conscious and deliberate choice of bringing Your presence into our lives. When we do this, we experience Your presence not only when we are engaged in formal study or prayer but even in our everyday tasks. The efforts we make toward recognizing Your hand in our lives will clear up the many clouds of misunderstanding and fear.

Your presence within the world is a hidden one. It cannot be readily perceived and recognized. We must delve and search, using our soul's light to guide us. We must first turn away from the many distractions that vie for our attention and discipline ourselves to become free of the many influences that abound within our environments. By training ourselves to focus instead on Your holiness and light, we become proper vessels capable of receiving the light of Your presence. This work requires our diligence and our attention, our love and our dedication. To be able to perceive and to recognize Your holy presence, we must engage our eyes and our ears, our minds and our hearts.

When we are able to fill our hearts with the awareness of God's presence, our fears and insecurities will naturally diminish. Love and awe of God will displace the negative feelings of anger or jealousy, lust or fear. The container of our hearts will leave no room to harbor the diseases of Godlessness.

Search your heart. Clear your mind. Guard your ears. Shield your eyes. Protect yourself within and without. Cleanse and prepare yourself to receive the illuminating and comforting light of the presence of your God. Make yourself into a vessel to receive His light, and feel the warmth and comfort of His protective presence.

May fear be banished from your heart.

May confusion be banished from your mind.

May you dwell in the security and safety of your Father's house, now and forever. Amen.

# Hidden Treasures

I long to find hidden treasures, treasures found deep in the sea, encased in their shells and hidden from view. I search beneath the ocean's surface, delving beneath the waves for the precious and royal treasures that await discovery. These lost treasures once adorned the world with their glory, but were exiled beneath the mighty waves of the ocean. Scattered on the ocean floor, they lie awaiting retrieval.

Most of us are unaware that these royal treasures exist. Many of us do not know or understand the glory that once existed, and without such knowledge, neither mourn their loss nor yearn for their retrieval. Despite our royal lineage, we have adapted to our lives as commoners. The glory of the past is a dim memory, known only to our souls. We are impoverished and have accustomed ourselves to our poverty. Our expectations have diminished and we are satisfied with cheap trinkets. Even our imaginations cannot go beyond the scope of our present poverty.

Let us open our eyes to the great glory of our regal tradition, learn and study about the greatness of our ancestors who were leaders of great spiritual stature and might. We must remember the pride and the glory of our great and holy Temple, reduced to ashes by our own blindness and ingratitude. Our stature as God's chosen ones was once apparent: all nations knew that a people brought out of slavery had been designated to be the royalty of the world. We were given great gifts of spiritual and material wealth, and our treasure houses were brimming with precious stones. We were a proud people; our leaders were awesome in their dignity and stature. We inspired the fear and awe of the nations around us. They knew that our Master was the true King of the world.

Let us recognize and mourn the loss of our greatness, and

understand that within us we carry the seeds of that greatness. We have the potential to reclaim our place as the ministers and representatives of our King in this world. We are still His chosen ones. We must yearn to retrieve what is hidden, dig and search for the golden vessels of our heritage and glory. As we weep for our current condition as disenfranchised heirs to the royal throne, let us focus on retrieving our inheritance and reestablishing our dominion. We have abdicated our royal birthright and have followed in the ways of the world.

Let us abandon our state of poverty, search out and reclaim the lost treasures. We must study our Guidebook and map our courses, searching tirelessly to locate the hidden wealth that was once our adornment and glory. We must open the shells that have formed barriers around these treasures, hiding them from view. We must not abandon our mission, give in to despair, or be complacent about accepting our diminished status and poverty. When the servants of the King are cast aside, the honor of their Master is also diminished. When we reclaim the lost treasures, we restore the presence of our King to His rightful place of honor in the world. We are responsible for His exile and we must provide the means for His return. Let us once again adorn ourselves in royal dress, take our places as ministers in the royal court, and restore the royal treasures to their rightful places. We must not rest until we have prepared the palace properly, making it fitting and proper for the return of our King.

May it be speedily in our days. Amen.

# Thanksgiving

The flow of blessing rises up from the earth, watering the land and quenching the thirst of all living creatures, an unending flow that sustains all of creation. From this stream of blessing we are able to grow, nourished and sustained by the life-giving waters.

Unaware of this process, we accept it as our entitlement, believing it is ours for the taking. We feel it is rightfully ours and take these blessings for granted. False pride tells us that we are important and worthy of all that the world has to offer. If we feel there is a lack in our lives, we consider it unfair, feeling that we deserve what we believe is good in the world and wondering why when we do not receive it.

We need rather to appreciate the constant and nourishing stream of blessing that gives us life and enables us to grow, and to feel humility at how fragile and dependent our lives really are. We need to open our hearts in thanksgiving and to recognize the gifts of life given to us each and every day.

We came into the world naked and bare; we would not have survived the day of our birth without the many blessings bestowed upon us. From that day on, we have been nourished and cared for, helped and provided for. Our health has been maintained, but have we acknowledged our Benefactor? Do we consider how fortunate we are to receive such great kindness and concern? Do we ponder what would happen should the great fountain of blessing, God forbid, ever dry up?

Let us open our minds in recognition of all that is done for us each day, and understand our responsibility of using the blessings of our lives wisely. When we recognize the importance of each moment of our lives and use our time and our resources wisely, we demonstrate our appreciation to our Creator Who has formed us and created us. Let us make our lives into a blessing and use its precious gifts to increase the flow of blessings into the world. Let us promote greater awareness of the Source of our blessings.

We are responsible for facilitating the flow of these blessings and enhancing its capacity. It is our important work to serve the Holy One Blessed be He, the Source of our lives, by digging wells to allow His waters of abundant blessing to nourish and to sustain the earth. Let us be faithful servants in carrying out this mission. Each of us is capable of bringing greater blessings into the world. Our Creator has a never-ending and abundant supply of life-giving water, but we must first recognize and appreciate the blessing of these sacred waters. We must dig our wells and guard them with great care, grateful to the great Source and Wellspring of our lives.

# The Seasoned Traveler

Barriers within disable us and keep us from proper functioning. Our task is to dislodge the impediments that prevent us from moving forward in our spiritual journeys.

Who are the gatekeepers of these barriers? How do we get past the obstructions that block us from our destinations? Sadly, we are our own gatekeepers. We have built the gates – gates of fear, of inertia, of passivity. Opening these gates means change and growth. We hide behind the tall fences we have erected, careful to keep the gates closed. We have a natural resistance to new directions and new challenges, and avoid what is unfamiliar, afraid to venture onto new paths and to travel to unfamiliar places.

We have accustomed ourselves to our current locations and are so comfortable and acclimated to them that we do not wish to disturb the status quo. Even if they are not comfortable, or even the cause of much discomfort, we still feel a strong attachment to what is familiar. It is an act of bravery to open a new gate; it takes faith and courage to move forward to unfamiliar places. We are so firmly rooted to our places that dislodging ourselves seems contrary to our natural tendency for the security of the familiar.

Our lives cannot and should not be sedentary, but rather, like those of travelers. Although we may need to stop from time to time to reflect on our current location and to give ourselves time to absorb the lessons of each place, we need to keep moving forward, never becoming too comfortable with or acclimated to any one stop in our journey. Even if we have come very far and traveled successfully through many places, we must never think that we have reached our final destination. There are always greater challenges and more difficult obstacles to be faced. However intimidating these obstacles may appear, we should not rest or refrain from continuing on.

As we break through each barrier and successfully overcome each impediment, we are strengthened by our accomplishments. Each time we are able to remove an obstruction and to go forward, we become seasoned and sturdy travelers who do not underestimate the journey's difficulties, but know that all obstacles can be overcome with planning, discipline, and determination. Experienced travelers know the great benefits and rewards their efforts bring, and also contemplate the shame and sorrow that they would feel if they had to sit at the side of the road and watch those who were once far behind pass them by.

Seasoned travelers do not rest, but greet each new barrier with strength and resolve. They look to each new challenge as an opportunity for growth and as a means to draw closer to their cherished goal of returning to their Father with the many accomplishments of their successful journey. They are aware that their Father in Heaven has sent them on the journey with love and the expectation of success. Successful travelers know the great importance of the journey and dedicate their lives to the fulfillment of their mission.

May we merit following in the ways of the many successful travelers who have preceded us.

May our efforts be tireless and filled with love and devotion.

May all the travelers within the world meet the challenges of their journeys with courage, dedication, and success. Amen.

# Potentials

*A drop of water. A wave of water pounding against the shore.*
*The power and majesty of a waterfall.*
*A grain of sand. The strength and power of a sandstorm.*
*The great expanse of a desert.*

Each small and seemingly insignificant element in the world can increase in force and strength. Each tall tree starts from a seedling. Each creature begins as a cell. Our origins are humble; our potential is great. A letter combined with other letters forms words. A word combined with other words becomes a book, and a library can be filled with these combinations of letters and words. The world is filled with potential. From a grain of sand a vast desert can be formed. From one letter, a whole Torah can be written. From one word, a world can be created. Strength can be derived from a small element of creation. We live in a world of tremendous potential for growth and life as well as for, God forbid, damage and destruction.

One drop of water combined with others fills our reservoirs. One drop of water combined with others can also, God forbid, cause a flood. A small flame combined with others can provide light and warmth. A small flame combined with others can also, God forbid cause a destructive fire. Nothing in creation is insignificant, nothing is superfluous. Each element in the physical world can grow and develop into a mighty force that can bring great benefit or, God forbid, cause great harm.

Human beings are the epitome of this natural dynamic and through their thoughts, words, and actions, can elevate themselves to positions of spiritual greatness and strength or, God forbid, lower themselves to positions of degradation and destructiveness. The majority of human beings reach neither of these two extremes. For most, there exists an internal struggle that at times leads them toward a path of holiness, and at others toward a path of impurity.

Joined with others to pray, we create a great flame of light and clarity; joined with others to mock or profane, we create flames of destruction and clouds of darkness. Each small action, each small word, each small thought is the equivalent of one small drop of water. In the course of a day we accumulate a river of thoughts, words, and actions that can become a reservoir of mitzvot or, God forbid, a flood of sins. When we multiply our days, the resulting benefit or damage we can create is tremendous. Each moment we can add drops either to the precious reservoir or God forbid, the destructive flood. Each day a substantial contribution is made by every individual toward the balance between benefit and damage. No drop of water is negligible. No word is without importance. We must understand the significance of all that we do, and never underestimate the outcomes of our deeds.

Every moment offers new opportunities, every situation brings its own challenges. At any moment we may, God forbid, stumble; at any moment we may, with His help, be elevated. A drop of water joins others to fill the ocean; a grain of sand joins others to fill the desert; a single flame joins others to create a conflagration. By the end of our days, each of our moments will join all the others in a significant accumulation. When the final accounting is done, will the balance combine as benefit and goodness or, God forbid, as damage and destruction? It is all important. Everything has its significance. The potential is there: The rest is up to us.

# Preparations

Let us prepare ourselves before the coming of Shabbat, and occupy ourselves with our preparations. What must we do to ensure that when it is time for the Shabbat Queen to arrive, all is prepared and ready to greet her?

All week long, let us look with an eye toward Shabbat. Shabbat is our opportunity to forge a deeper connection between our physical selves and our spiritual selves, between ourselves and the Holy One Blessed be He. How can we make the most of this opportunity? Shabbat is the culmination of our spiritual preparations for the week, and our source of spiritual enrichment for the upcoming week. To derive benefit from the spiritual nourishment of Shabbat, we need to ready ourselves and our households to receive our royal visitor.

When you are given the great opportunity of an audience with the spiritual presence and holiness of the Shabbat Queen, you must be properly prepared to greet her. Learn how to behave in her majestic presence. Make the Shabbat Queen feel welcome in your heart and in your home with speech that is proper and respectful. Your royal guest will not feel comfortable staying in a home lacking in words of Torah. Show your gratitude and appreciation for having the honor of her presence.

The presence of Shabbat can bring many blessings to your home if you are prepared to receive them. During the week we engage in many preparations: We buy and prepare our food, wash our clothes, and clean our houses; we purchase our candles and polish our candlesticks. All of the many ways in which we prepare properly for our Shabbat guest demonstrates the great care and concern we have to be ready for her arrival. In addition to our many physical preparations to welcome the Shabbat Queen and make her comfortable in our homes, we must also make spiritual preparations for her visit. If we spend our weekdays absorbed only in our businesses, chores, and everyday concerns, we will not be spiritually prepared to welcome her.

During the week, we must feel the yearning in our souls for the spiritual nourishment that only Shabbat can provide, and be aware of what is lacking within when we are not connected to the holiness of Shabbat. From within and without we are bereft of her special qualities during the course of our week: Recognize this lack and anticipate with great expectation the arrival of our most cherished and honored guest.

We must study the Torah portion of the week to derive the special lessons that this particular Shabbat comes to teach us, and review the laws of Shabbat to ensure that all our actions are fitting and proper in her presence. Let us be careful to provide the Shabbat Queen with accommodations befitting her lofty stature and sensibilities. Our elevation of Shabbat elevates us. Only when we properly prepare ourselves to welcome the Shabbat Queen will we be able to receive her great blessings. Our homes will then be infused with her holiness. The opportunities and blessings of Shabbat are awesome, its resources are bountiful, but we must recognize these resources and their opportunities to properly benefit from them. Shabbat is the fount from which great waters flow. Let us ready ourselves to receive these healing and nourishing waters, and make ourselves into reservoirs to keep and store these precious waters.

Please help me, dear God, to recognize and to appreciate Your great source of blessing.

Please help me, dear God, to prepare myself properly to receive Your precious gift.

Please help me, dear God, to be able to drink and to find refreshment from the blessings of Your living waters. Amen.

# Our Life's Blood

As the blood flows forth from the beating heart that pumps it through the organs and limbs of the body, the body becomes nourished. This constant flow of life-giving blood supports the many systems and functions of life. Failure in the proper flow, from defect or blockage, can result in disease or even death to the body. The constant flow of this vital fluid cannot be interrupted or stopped at any place in its journey through the body.

The mitzvot of the Torah are the life-sustaining fluid of our spiritual lives that nourishes and gives energy to our souls. For our souls to function in health and vitality, we must receive the life-sustaining blood of the mitzvot. When, God forbid, blockage or damage impedes the proper flow of the mitzvot to our spiritual organs and limbs, our souls become diseased and lifeless. Just as our bodies require a constant flow of blood, so too are our souls in constant need of mitzvot.

If we only involve ourselves in some mitzvot while neglecting others, we may become spiritually anemic and weak. Our life source needs the various nutrients that different mitzvot can provide. A soul lacking in the constant flow of these various spiritual nutrients will weaken, and her ability to connect with her Godly image will be impaired. Just as we cannot live a single moment without the proper functioning of our circulatory systems, so too do our souls need constant mitzvot to maintain the health and proper functioning of our souls.

Our souls are our spiritual life source. When, God forbid, we lose our connection to our spiritual selves, we cut ourselves off from our true source. Like a tree uprooted from the earth, its source of nourishment and life, our spiritual leaves and branches can wither and become lifeless if we lose our connection to the roots of our being.

We feed our bodies so that our blood can receive proper nourishment; so too, must we feed our souls with the nourishment of the mitzvot. If we only eat one kind of food, our bodies will not receive the various nutrients required for proper health; so too, we need more than one mitzvah to maintain our spiritual health. The greater the variety of mitzvot, the better able our spiritual organs and limbs will be to function in harmony and in health. Common wisdom tells us that eating once a week, or even once a day, will not provide our bodies with sufficient energy to function at an optimal level; so too, mitzvot done sporadically will not be sufficient to enliven and to sustain our spiritual beings properly.

Mitzvot are our life's blood. Just as God has given all creatures food to sustain their health and growth, so too, through His Torah has God given us mitzvot to sustain our spiritual health and growth. The available bounty of mitzvot is beyond measure, the opportunities for development, abundant: There is no limit to how high the branches of your tree can reach when planted firmly in the rich soil of Torah and nourished by the observance of mitzvot.

We must keep our spiritual hearts strong, the blood rich and flowing. Let us constantly nourish ourselves with the life-sustaining and spiritually enriching mitzvot of the Torah.

# Coal and Diamonds

The flame attaches itself to a piece of coal. From the darkness of this black rock, fire emanates. From the coal's hard surface, warmth issues forth, flames so delicate, so ethereal in contrast to the dense coal. Yet the fire needs this black rock as a source of fuel to sustain its existence in this world. The ethereal fire is inextricably linked to the dense coal.

Our world is replete with examples of this basic contrast. All around us we see the solidity of our world integrally linked with spirituality. Our senses perceive and interact with the many forms of physical life that surround us, but it is the flame of our souls that elevates that physicality to holiness.

When we take the dark coal of our physical existence and dedicate it to a spiritual purpose, it becomes as clear and bright as the shimmering, reflective surface of a diamond. The material world is transformed and elevated whenever we attach the name of God to the physical elements of existence. Unseen flames of light and splendor emanate whenever we sanctify the elements of the world with God's never-ending stream of blessing. By uniting these elements with God's name, we become agents in transforming and infusing them with the holiness of spiritual light.

Human beings are unique in their ability to bring forth light from this dense and opaque physical world. No other creation, whether physical or spiritual, has this unique capability to draw spiritual influence down from the heavens. Of all the many material things that we can transform and infuse with holiness, it is we ourselves who can undergo the greatest of transformations. Through the vehicle of our souls, our dense, material bodies can be elevated to great spiritual eminence. The coal of our earthly being has the potential to shine forth with the radiance of its hidden spiritual essence, the dense black rock becoming a multifaceted, brilliant diamond.

It is within our power to transform ourselves and all that surrounds us by attaching ourselves to the channels of blessing and spiritual flow. Our task is awesome. Our capabilities are tremendous, and our ability to influence and to affect the world around us is great. When we allow ourselves to become conduits for God's spiritual influence, and attach ourselves wholeheartedly to the service of our Creator, aligning our will to the will of our God, we bring forth the bounty of God's heavenly blessing, the great spiritual light of peace and clarity hidden within all of creation. Through our efforts, the world can be transformed from the darkness of opaque coal to the prismatic transparence of diamonds.

May we recognize our great potential.

May we humbly submit ourselves to the will of our Creator.

May we serve as vehicles to bring down heavenly sustenance to our world. Amen.

# Will and Desire

When we attach our will and determination to a specific goal, we promote that goal to a place of prominence by making time for and devoting our energy and resources to what is important to us. Once we have set our priorities, our lives revolve around these goals. We make conscious and unconscious decisions to pursue these goals whenever given the opportunity, and train ourselves to be responsive to opportunities that help us to attain our goals.

For example, if our goal is to acquire a position of status and honor, whenever we recognize an opportunity to enhance our status, we will be sure to make use of the opportunity. Other opportunities present at the same time will be ignored, or perhaps not even recognized, in our quest for greater status. We establish a hierarchy of desires and exert our will toward the attainment to those desires. We pursue those goals to which our hearts have become attached.

We can either allow the desires of our hearts to direct our thoughts and actions, or we can use our intellects to determine the direction that we follow. The priorities of our hearts must be guided by the discipline of our minds, for without proper direction, our hearts tend to follow the course of our evil inclination. We have many instincts and character traits that can lead us along misleading and futile paths when left unchecked and undisciplined.

Our hearts need to be trained to understand the long-term benefits or, God forbid, the long-term damage that can be inflicted once we embark on a given course. Once we have accustomed ourselves to a particular path, it becomes increasingly difficult to leave it to follow a different one. We use our intellects to establish our priorities. We must plan and develop the course that we will follow and be careful not to deviate from it. The longer we travel these paths, the more habituated our hearts become to them. They come to desire what brings them closer to their goal, and conversely, learn to avoid what hinders their progress. A heart trained on a path of kindness and good deeds naturally desires and seeks opportunities to do these mitzvot. Conversely, a heart directed toward haughtincss and status-seeking, God forbid, searches for opportunities to further those goals.

In the absence of proper training and development, the evil inclination always tries to exert influence over our hearts, leading us away from our proper paths. Even a heart that has been trained in the way of Torah and mitzvot can be lead astray by the many tricks of the evil inclination. These traps are suited to accommodate the spiritual level of each individual. Obvious traps won't be successful with those who have developed their spiritual level of awareness to recognize and to avoid them. However, the evil inclination understands that these individuals have attained a more advanced level and lays more subtle traps that are not as easily seen or avoided. Just as an experienced master of chess will not be easily fooled by elementary strategies, so too, the evil inclination knows its opponents and designs strategies accordingly.

We need to strengthen our will constantly to pursue the desires of our good inclination. Our adversary is clever, but we have the ability to recognize and avoid its many traps. By accustoming ourselves to a Torah path, by our conscious efforts in doing mitzvot, and by continually calling to our God for His help and encouragement, the will of our good inclination can and will be victorious.

Let us keep our eyes focused on our goal.

Let us accustom our hearts to their proper paths.

Let us move our feet in the direction that will lead us to our God. Amen.

# Arrogance

It is risky to plunge headfirst into the water without knowing its depth or what lies beneath. Rocks or dangerous sea life may await you. We may consider ourselves experienced divers who have emerged unharmed many times from new and uncharted territory. We may think that our special talents and abilities make us invulnerable to dangers beneath the surface of the sea, yet the greatest danger we face is our arrogance.

When we rely only on our own strength and understanding, we are prone to many mistakes in judgment. By trusting only in our own abilities and our own ideologies, we can come, God forbid, to an idolatory of self and consider ourselves invincible, allowing our egos to reign supreme. We then believe in our superiority over all others and view them as misguided or lacking in understanding. We make the words of the Torah subservient to our own wishes and desires, and allow our egos to wear the crown of sovereignty. We become deaf to any outside counsel.

By following this course, our arrogance eventually plunges us, unthinking, into dangerous waters. We become so falsely self-assured that our souls are in jeopardy. This process gains strength over time: Step by step, we become bolder in our egocentricity, and less and less responsive to the call of the Torah and the voices of our souls. We do not exercise caution in our speech or contemplate our actions beforehand. We become oblivious to the sensitivities of anyone but ourselves: Only our opinions are correct. Our wants and desires take precedence over the needs of others, and we view other people in terms of their benefit to us. The bounty of the world exists solely for our personal pleasure and use, and we expect the world to be responsive to our wills and desires. This is an attitude that inevitably leads to misfortune and sorrow.

Our Creator created the world with great loving kindness; He built its structure to function in an optimal way through the loving kindness of His people. When we do not follow the master plan of God's Torah, we cause damage to the foundations of existence: All human beings need to follow His guiding principles of kindness, love, compassion, sensitivity, justice, and concern for others. When we ignore these basic principles, we cause, God forbid, damage to the very existence of our world.

Time and again throughout history we have examples of the pain and suffering caused by arrogance. Lack of concern for others in the quest to satisfy the desires of the ego has caused untold division and strife. When we follow the path of arrogance, we put ourselves and those around us in peril. When we exalt our egos above all else, we plunge into uncharted waters without consideration for the ramifications of our actions.

Let us maintain firm limitations on the desires of our ego.

Let us act at all times with sensitivity, kindness, and concern.

Let us be mindful, always, of following in the path to our God. Amen.

# The Flow of Our Lives

I hear the sounds of the river as it rushes downstream. The water follows the contours of the rock formations, its fluidity allowing it to be flexible and to adjust to the many obstacles in its path. As it makes its way over and around fallen branches and stones, it moves steadily toward its destination.

The nature of life is to follow and to flow in a given direction. The constant cycles inherent in all of life repeat themselves over time. Some have short spans, some have longer ones, but the cycles are ceaseless. We, too, are a part of a cycle of movement and change, and must go in our directions, adjusting to whatever obstacles we encounter on our paths. We remain a part of the cycle of life even when we try to deviate from it.

Water goes its own way when undeterred. We, however, may hesitate or decide to stop the flow of our lives; we may even try to go backwards. We may try to interfere with or to reverse the flow by trying to go against the current and traveling upstream. We may think we can go to places that are not our true destinations. We may even try to change the course of the flow of our lives. All such efforts, however, will be fruitless. Even though we can create for ourselves an illusion of success, we can never truly succeed in traveling in directions in which we were not meant to travel. We may be stubborn, we may muster all our strength and determination, but we can never attain what is not our portion.

We need to examine the flow of our lives and to understand the direction in which its current is going. When we encounter obstacles in our way, we must learn to circumvent them and to continue on. True success can only come by following the natural flow of our lives, a pattern that is unique for each individual. No two journeys follow the same itinerary. Only the natural flow will lead us in our proper directions.

Once we understand the pattern and flow of our lives, we can achieve maximal results by uniting our potentials to our circumstances. We need to examine our natures, talents, abilities, and deficiencies, and use the opportunities that our journeys provide, instead of fighting the natural current of our lives. We must examine the itinerary of our journey, and then live our days in conformity to it. Only by doing so will we be able to bring ourselves closer to our destinations. It is important to understand and to accept both the opportunities and the limitations of our journeys.

The sound of the river traveling downstream calls to me, "Come follow," beckoning me to walk the unique path that I have been given, to accept its challenge and to leave behind my hesitations and fears. I give myself up to the call of my future with joy, courage, and trust, going forward, even though I may not know what lies ahead, following the flow and pattern that is my life.

May God grant us the wisdom to recognize our true directions.

May God strengthen us to follow our true courses.

May we all join together in diversity and in unification. Amen.

# The Baker

Within your tent, the bread is prepared. The flour requires careful sifting, the dough, careful kneading. Use pure and wholesome grain with no trace of foreign elements so that the bread you consume will provide you with all the nutrients needed for your health and growth. Knead the dough well with clean hands, and follow the recipe precisely. You must know how long the dough takes to rise and exactly how long it needs to bake. This process requires your attention and your love. Prepare your bread properly and with a joyful heart, and it will be well baked, nourishing, and delicious.

You are meant to share your bread with the hungry, with those who, traveling by your tent and smelling the fragrant aroma coming from within, become acutely aware of their own hunger. When they see the beautiful loaves you have baked, they will realize their own deprivation. Establish your tent and then open it up, sharing the fruits of your labor with hungry travelers in need of sustenance.

It took you years to learn the recipe. Only after many mistakes and wasted effort were you able to produce nourishing bread. Even though there are many bakers more experienced and skilled, you have mastered the basic techniques. It will take you a lifetime to perfect your bread, but don't despair: There is much joy in the learning.

You are a baker and a host. These are the jobs you are meant to do. Do your work with enthusiasm. Do your work with love. Bring pride and your best efforts to your work each day. Provide yourself and those around you with nourishment and sustenance. Feed yourself well and you will be able to feed others. Share the lessons you have learned with others so they can learn to prepare their own bread and become bakers, too. We are all following the same recipe, yet the bread that each of us produces is different from anyone else's. Each contribution is unique.

Learn your craft well and practice it wholeheartedly. The light of your soul will find happiness, and the world around you will radiate with the love and attention you have brought to your work. Stay focused and don't become discouraged by mistakes. With love, determination, and God's help, your efforts will be productive, your days will be full, and you will become blessed in the eyes of your Creator.

# A Voyage Through Rough Seas

A small boat travels across a stormy ocean, the waves high and the sky dark with clouds; powerful waves easily toss and turn the boat. The captain knows the strength of the waves and the force of the storms of wind and rain that may at any time rock his tiny boat, yet he is not afraid. He keeps his hands confidently on the wheel and looks ahead with calm eyes and heart, secure, and unwavering in his security. He knows that the rains and wind will neither change his course nor keep him from his destination. Storms may threaten, waves may tower around him, but the captain remains calm and secure at his post.

He knows that the power of the sea and the skies are only servants of their Master; these elements do not control and have no power over the fate of his boat. He is confident in the knowledge that without the order and direction of their Master, they are weak and powerless. He does not fear the rages of wind and water because he trusts in the goodness and justness of their Creator. He knows that only by the will of God will his tiny boat be able to travel securely through rough seas, and that his faith and trust in God will keep him safe. His only real and appropriate fear is that of his own sins.

The captain steers his small ship with open eyes; in his heart he keeps the constant remembrance of Who his Master is and Who it is he must always serve. He knows that his job is to keep his boat firmly on its course, and that if he does so with effort and concentration, he has nothing to fear from storms or the dangers of the high seas.

Our Master gives us life and goodness; He wants us to follow His direction and guidance and to serve Him in joy and gratitude. Our God is always there to guard and to protect us, to guide us through all storms and rough seas. Like the captain of the ship, our only fear should be our lack of commitment to His precious Torah and mitzvot, our lack of effort in guarding ourselves from sin, and our own blindness. Let us trust completely in our Master and be concerned only about our own wrongdoing.

May we be able to sail our ships safely through dangerous and storm-tossed waters.

May we merit the help and protection of our Master.

May we always remember the importance of our voyages. Amen.

# The Date Tree

Each year the date tree puts forth new branches that grow in size and in strength and bring forth fruit. The branches are cut off at the end of the season and a new generation replaces the old. When we look at the date tree we see the remnants of the former generations; from these, new life sprouts forth, new branches grow. Each generation grows higher, closer to the sky, yet remains firmly connected to its roots.

Each tree is the result of many generations that brought forth their bounty and then made way for the future. Like the date tree, we represent the current generation of branches. It is now our turn to take our places on the tree, to bring forth fruit, and then to leave, making way for the next generation. Each successive generation brings new strength and growth; each new branch builds on the foundation of previous generations.

Our current place developed from the tree of our forefathers. The seed was planted by our forefather Abraham, who planted it by the Wellspring of Living Waters; the seed was guarded and protected by his son, Isaac. The next stage of development, represented by Jacob, was then ready to bear fruit. From the third generation, a bountiful harvest blossomed forth from twelve strong branches. This ancient tree has endured many tempests during its existence on earth. Despite repeated assaults, the strength of its roots has sustained the tree with the courage and fortitude to continue to grow higher.

We belong to the current generation of branches from this ancient tree, a continuation of a noble line. From the seed of Abraham and through the many branches that preceded us and stood fast in their determination to continue the legacy, we have survived and stand tall.

The task of each generation is to remain steadfastly connected to its roots, deriving nourishment from the same Wellspring that made possible the growth of the seed of Abraham. Only because Abraham planted his seed by the Living Waters of Torah was the tree able to take root and to grow. This same Wellspring has sustained the tree of the children of Israel throughout its history.

We draw sustenance from this Wellspring just as did our ancestors; it is the Source of our vitality. Our branches connect deeply to the generations before us that grew, developed, and brought forth their fruit. As extensions of this great tradition and the current guardians of its great and holy legacy, let us be sturdy offshoots of this noble tradition. Let us keep our generation of branches healthy by drinking heartily from the waters of Torah, ensuring that our precious legacy remains strong. It is our turn to be guardians of this most precious tree. Let us assume the responsibility of preserving and watching over our precious Tree of Life, the one true Source of holiness in the world.

# The Illuminating Light

All living things reach for the light. Tree branches reach toward the sky; flower petals open to the sun. We seek the light, which clarifies and illuminates, enlivens and regenerates. The golden rays of sunshine in a cloudless sky beckon me to come closer, enticing me out of my shelter to bask in their light.

I need the nourishing light of growth and understanding each day of my life, dear Lord. Only in such clear and unobstructed light can I bring myself closer to Your presence. In a dense forest it is difficult to see the light, to feel its warmth above the many tall trees. When clouds come, it becomes even more difficult to receive the healing light, but I still search for it, following paths through the forest to greater visibility. I search constantly for places with less obstruction and greater clarity, places of light.

Inside each of us is a light that yearns to be part of the greater light of the heavens. Our small candles long to connect to their Source and with other candles to increase the common light. When we bring our candles together, we can generate a greater light from within.

Darkness within causes anger. It causes dissension and strife; it causes separation. We become lost to ourselves, to others, and to God, our great Source of light. Darkness is a place of laziness where we try to hide from God and the work He has assigned us. We think that if we hide in dark places we will not be seen, and that God will not notice that we have been avoiding our studies, neglecting our assignments.

To the eyes of God there are no hiding places; there is no place beyond His vision and authority. To hide is pointless and self-defeating. We must step out into the sunshine. Our dark hiding places afford us no security and only keep us groping blindly and shivering with cold. The light within us grows dim; our ability to discern and to evaluate properly diminishes and we lose our ability to distinguish what is around us. Our inner lights no longer illuminate our hearts and our minds.

Avoiding the precious and holy light estranges us from our God, and correspondingly, from ourselves. Unable to see the damage we do to our souls when we hide from the heavenly light, we lose our capacity to distinguish what is correct from what is incorrect. We grope in the darkness, bumping into one obstacle after another, hurting ourselves over and over again without even being aware of the injuries we are inflicting.

Light is essential to our beings: We are creatures of the light. When we distance ourselves from the holy light, we endanger our very lives. Our existence depends on our ability to see clearly and to receive the warmth and loving light of our God. When we accustom ourselves to places of darkness, we diminish our ability to perceive and to understand, causing damage to ourselves and to those around us through our ignorance. The light within becomes layered with misperceptions, reducing our ability to connect to our own source of holiness.

We must open our eyes and move our feet, leave our dark place in the forest and search tirelessly and unceasingly for greater clarity of perception. Let us join with others who are pursuing the path that will lead us all to the glorious light of Torah understanding. By joining our candles with those of others, the combined light will produce an even greater illumination.

As guardians of the flame within, we can bring greater light into our world. By allowing the healing, holy light to illuminate us, we reflect the holy light from heaven. By connecting our small candles to the great and mighty flame of our Father, we become light keepers in the service of our Father the King.

We all have this awesome potential; we all harbor a source of light and wisdom within. It is up to us to recognize this source and to keep it burning brightly by seeking clarity, enabling ourselves to grow and to reach higher toward the light. Let us each do our part to dispel the darkness by increasing the lights of Torah and mitzvah observance in the world.

We were born to be light keepers. Our work is to guard and to enhance the bright light of Godliness so that it can enlighten our world.

May we merit to see and to experience this enlightenment soon in our days. Amen.

# Searching for the Wind

The breath of life, like the wind, is sensed but not seen. We see waves blown by the wind but not the wind. We can hear the rustling of leaves, we feel the breeze blowing on our faces, but we cannot see the breeze itself. We observe the myriad of actions and reactions of life all around us, the ceaseless activity of all living things. It is the Generator of life that we do not see.

We feel, sense, and see the pulse and movement of our world, but not the Hand that guides, directs, and sustains all of creation. It is by using our discerning hearts and our probing minds that we can come to some understanding of this guiding and loving Hand. It is with our inner eyes that we can perceive the origins of our existence. We must search within to understand and to experience the true nature of our lives, and use our inner light to explore and to follow the path that leads to spiritual awareness.

Like the air we breathe, our spiritual breath is within and all around us, and like the air, we cannot see it. When we see ripples on the surface of the water, we realize there is a force that causes its movement, yet we often fail to contemplate the Life Force that is everywhere and the basis of everything. We need to search for and to examine this wind, to explore what we sense but cannot see. Our minds tell us there is a reason that leaves move in the air, and we must search for it. We are not here just to feel and to experience the wind that blows, but to develop an understanding of, and a connection with its Source.

Within each of us is a wind that perceives the wind that surrounds us. A small wind within us connects to the mighty Wind that breathes life into all living things. It is not enough to sit still and experience this wind. We must discover the nature of this wind and its Source. Human nature is not like the other forms of natural life. For birds, it is sufficient for them to know that wind is what aids them in their flight; for us that knowledge is not enough.

We must use the higher resources of our souls to learn and to grow in our knowledge of the vivifying winds of our spiritual existence. Our purpose is to explore and to understand the inner, spiritual dimension that underlies our physical existence. Even with the limitations of our physical life, we have the ability to delve into our spiritual natures. Let us follow the path that will bring us closer to the Source of our lives. We must look carefully; we must dig deeply. We must use all of the resources that we have been given, searching tirelessly to understand the Breath of Life that sustains us all.

# Eclipse

During a solar eclipse it appears to us as if the moon and the sun are the same size, and as if the darkness of the moon equals the sun's brightness. We know that these perceptions are illusions, for the sun is actually many times the size of the moon. Although the moon is positioned so that, to our view, it is blocking the sun, we know that in reality the moon cannot in any way affect the light and heat generated by the sun.

We attribute a similar, deceptive illusion to the darkness of evil. Some people mistakenly think the darkness of evil can, God forbid, eclipse the great spiritual light of Torah, but it is only the illusion of darkness that they perceive. Evil derives its existence from their belief in it. Just as the moon can in no way diminish the light of the sun, so evil is powerless to affect the great spiritual light of Torah. The perception of evil derives from our attachment to that belief, its existence predicated on our acceptance of an illusion.

Nothing in creation can, God forbid, affect or diminish God's spiritual light. When we create barriers between ourselves and our God by turning away from the light of Torah, we create an eclipse. It is because of our belief in the profane and our adherence to non-Torah values that a spiritual eclipse seems to appear. To those who know and understand the truth of God's light, there can never be a blockage or diminishment of the Light. By attaching ourselves to false concepts and ideologies, we create the illusion of darkness. Our vision becomes dim when we move away from the path of Torah.

The light of our souls also seems eclipsed when we move toward false gods. But just as the life-sustaining light of our Creator can never be diminished, neither can the light of our souls ever be dimmed. We create our own barriers, our own darkness. We give credence to the illusion that there is, God forbid, no light that emanates from our souls.

Primitive peoples believe that the moon exerts an influence over the sun. People who lack an understanding of Torah believe that God's holy light can be affected, God forbid, by the shades of evil. It is this belief that causes despair, this lack of understanding that causes estrangement from our God. It is we who give strength to the mistaken belief in the power of evil. It is we who perpetuate this primitive way of thinking.

We must recognize always the truth of God's everlasting light and never support the false ideology of evil. Our perception of evil comes from our own lack of proper understanding, and our perception of an eclipse of God's light is the deception of our evil inclination. When we adhere to this deception, we estrange ourselves from God and alienate our own souls. We make the evil inclination's illusion our reality.

Let us keep our eyes open and focused on God's heavenly light.

Let us overcome the deceptive illusions of our evil inclination.

Let us properly prepare ourselves to receive the great light of Torah into our hearts. Amen.

# Building Houses

*To sit in the house of God.*
*To be able to sit securely and peacefully in His House.*
*To dwell safely within the walls of His Divine Presence.*

We seek respite from the winds and rains in our lives, for shelter to protect us from the effects of its many storms. Often, we avail ourselves of only temporary refuges, made of flimsy construction and inferior materials. Such places are available everywhere and easily procured. We don't have to expend much time or effort in acquiring such temporary shelters.

To establish a shelter of substance and fortitude, however, we must labor in its construction, establishing a firm foundation with the wisdom of the Torah as our blueprint. Building our sturdy houses is a labor of love and dedication. It takes a lifetime commitment to build and to maintain such a house, and to keep it in good repair.

Our houses shelter us from the storm, from strong winds and heavy rains; they are our places of rest and respite from the pressures and difficulties we meet with day in and day out. Our houses are our sanctuaries. So, too, must the spiritual houses that we build protect us from life's storms and provide us with a dwelling place under God's protection. There we can find the peace and security necessary to connect with our Creator. Without a secure and spiritual dwelling we may, God forbid, fall prey to the winds and storms of our days on this earth.

We must plan ahead. When the storms come, let us not take refuge in any available shelter, but rather prepare ourselves by constructing a house of strength and endurance, and spend time each day in its maintenance. We must never allow our house to fall into ruin and disrepair. Our lifelong task is to establish a dwelling from which we can call on our God and be available to receive His answer: A place of devotion, of dedication, of connection.

Build this house on a foundation of trust, with bricks composed of faith, and a roof secured with love and devotion. Let its many windows allow God's holy light to enter. A house built with the wisdom of the Torah and dedicated to the service of the Holy One Blessed be He will be, with His help, a house that will endure forever.

May we take great care in the building of our houses.

May we use the sturdy materials of faith and love.

May our houses endure in strength, in purpose, and in the service of our Lord. Amen.

# A Clear Path

The path is overgrown. Weeds, branches, and thickets obscure the way. Before you can make your way through the forest, you must clear the path. The debris that covers the pathways is confusing and you can easily lose your way. Take care to remove whatever obstructs your vision: Within the dark and dense forest, it is easy to be misled.

Do not walk where your path is obscured. Hidden dangers lurk beneath the leaves and underbrush, and it is hard to protect yourself from unseen predators lying in wait. Inspect the way carefully before you travel: A path that appears safe may contain pitfalls and swamps lurking beneath the surface. Be careful where you step.

Use your inner light to guide you. Do not wander through the forest unprepared: check the maps of the area before you venture forth. Study the best ways to navigate dangerous terrain. Prepare yourself each day for that day's journey, and fortify yourself to meet its unexpected challenges. Do not wait until the unexpected presents itself before determining your course of action. Study and learn well about all the potential dangers that are to be found within the forest.

Stop regularly in your travels and ask your Father to guide you on your way. Call on Him for help and direction. Consult your Guidebook each day so that you do not wander off in the wrong direction. Do not be lulled into the false security of thinking that you have become an experienced traveler who knows well all the twists and turns of the forest's paths. Even if you have applied yourself diligently to your studies, continue to strive for ever-greater clarity and wisdom. All travelers, whatever their level of experience and understanding, must be careful and vigilant.

Even seasoned travelers encounter new and more subtle dangers yet unrevealed.

The creatures of the forest are clever and know your weaknesses well: Guard yourself from their snares and schemes; prepare yourself for their dangerous traps. Plan in advance your response to the challenges that each day brings.

It is difficult for any traveler to journey through the forest without sustaining an injury, but the rewards of a completed journey are beyond measure. With careful planning, preparation, and God's help, your journey through the forest will be successful.

May we merit to journey through life with minimal injury and abundant reward.

May we navigate safely through the many dangerous pathways.

May our Father in Heaven be pleased with our efforts. Amen.

# Coming Back

You had good intentions. You knew your goals and where you were headed. You began this past year's journey with a sense of renewal and purpose. You made use of the opportunities given to you during last year's High Holy Days and you made a fresh start. You looked ahead to a year that you hoped would be filled with purpose and accomplishment. You felt that prayer and the cleansing effects of your repentance had provided you with a new beginning. You believed that your heartfelt prayers had been accepted, and that you had been granted a new year of opportunities for growth and development.

Now you are looking back, reflecting on the success and failure of your efforts. You believe that overall progress was made, but are distressed at the number of times you strayed from your path. You feel sad for the times that you were distracted and veered off onto strange roads because you were not paying attention to the road signs or had not consulted your maps. Sometimes the lapse was momentary and you quickly returned to the proper road, but at other times you just continued on mindlessly in your lost direction.

The good intentions and resolutions formulated in the month of Tishrei were sometimes forgotten in the months of Kislev and Tammuz. The momentum generated at the beginning of the year lost some of its energy as the year progressed. As you followed your itinerary during this past year's journey, you sometimes became lax in the fulfillment of your tasks. You acquiesced to your desire to stop at the side of the road, or you forgot the lessons you had been taught and had to recognize and take responsibility for your mistakes.

How do we guard against these mistakes, this laxity, these

distractions that grab our attention and lure us away from our paths? How can we ensure that the errors of one year will not be repeated the next? How can we maintain the level of enthusiasm and motivation that we feel as we leave our *succot* (tabernacles) for the last time, rejoicing in the new opportunities to serve God in the coming year? How can we make the best use of these opportunities?

Success in our service depends on our connection with the Holy One Blessed be He. Our level of awareness and our closeness to our Creator is our best defense against sin. We connect to the Source of all when we open up our hearts in prayer, when we open up our minds with Torah study, when we maintain recognition of our spiritual beings. The more connected we are to Him, the less chance there is for distraction. When we focus on our soul's yearning to be closer to her Source, we increase our spiritual awareness and guard against the temptations all around us. When our minds and hearts are directed toward the yearnings of our souls, we aren't tempted to follow strange paths or to stop at the side of the road.

Our sins result from inattention to our relationship with God. Without a conscious and determined effort to become closer to our God, we look to worldly distractions to satisfy our longings. The love and devotion that should be directed toward Him finds, God forbid, other ways to satisfy these longings. Staying focused on spiritual development is not automatic; it requires our best efforts and attention. When we stray from the direction in which our souls yearn to travel, we become lost in the forest of our earthly desires. This path leads us further away from our God, and in our confusion and darkness, we commit errors of judgment.

The path that leads us toward God is one of light and illumination; the path that leads us way from God is one of darkness and sin. In this new year, at this new beginning, let us resolve to develop and to maintain our connection to the Holy One Blessed be He. Let us strive to heighten our awareness of His presence, and to fully use His holy light. He is available to all, and He yearns for the return of us, His children. Let us return and move closer to Him. Our God is a God of forgiveness, and He awaits our heartfelt return to His service with great anticipation.

In this sacred and auspicious time, may we turn away from our lost paths.

May we avail ourselves of our Creator's divine favor and mercy.

May we resolve in our hearts to follow the yearnings of our souls.

May we merit in this new year to experience a closer connection and attachment to our Lord and Creator Blessed be He. Amen.

# Colors

Many colors make up the autumnal landscape. Each leaf has its distinct shape and hue. I love them all – the yellow leaves, the brown ones, the red. The diversity of life enriches us. Variations of color fill the sky in joyful tribute to their Creator. Judging which color is best diminishes them all. Appreciation of each one's unique beauty opens our hearts to the wonder of God.

Let us study the complexity of the world in which we now live: There are many lessons to be learned. Each leaf has a purpose, each color is important. The world has its order and its natural way of functioning. Within the wonder of nature we find the hand of God. The world's ways are balance, growth, and change. The interrelationships among natural elements make each moment of existence unique and wondrous to behold. The harmony of each element acting and interacting with others in countless ways is astonishing in its diversity.

As human beings, we are partners in the great workings of this world. We have the awesome responsibility either to perfect or, God forbid, to damage our world. Creatures go through cycles of life and death, making the world neither better nor worse because of their existence; but we, through our thoughts, efforts, and accomplishments, can truly change all of creation.

Our forefather Abraham brought great blessings to the world; Pharaoh brought great damage. Within the scope of our life's circumstances, we can follow the path of Abraham or, God forbid, of Pharaoh. Any one person can bring us all closer to redemption or, God forbid, take us further from it. God offers us the gift of choice, the great opportunity of working in His service to perfect the world. We have the ability to use the resources and opportunities we have and through our acts of sanctification, bring ourselves and the entire world closer to clarity and holiness. As we appreciate the wonders of this world, let us understand the ramifications of our actions and the capacity we have, God forbid, to cause damage.

Your work is important: You are in the service of the King. Do not shirk your responsibilities. Do not waste this precious time. Use the opportunities of your life to the best of your ability. Your contribution is significant and can change the balance of all of creation. Follow the example of Abraham: Be steadfast in your service. Do not be discouraged by difficulty, and believe with a full heart in the goodness of your Creator.

Each leaf has a distinctive color. Each creation has a specific purpose. Everything is both unique and a part of the whole of creation. Contribute according to your capacity, according to your unique abilities. Do your part to bring harmony and the peace of redemption to our world. Underestimate neither your work nor your ability to do it. The world awaits your contribution, your dedication, and your love.

# Dedication

Dedicate what has been given to you as a gift. Offer yourself, all that you are and all that you have, to the service of your Creator. To come closer to your God, make the commitment to give yourself wholly to His service. Only what has been designated for holiness can come close to holiness: What is mundane cannot approach. To bring yourself as an offering, you must be without blemish. You must make yourself as pure as the oil from the first pressing of olives. You must be free from defect or flaw, all elements foreign to holiness removed if you truly desire to bring yourself closer to your God. It is within your capability.

We have incorporated much of the world that surrounds us. We have brought foreign concepts and ideologies into our houses. We have assimilated the idolatrous ways and customs of our environment into our beings, diminishing the light of our beautiful souls. These foreign concepts act as shades and separate us from the holiness within, creating barriers that keep us distant from our God. We have become estranged from our own souls, alienated from our God. The flame of holiness that burns inside of us yearns to connect to its Source. Our work is to remove barriers, to guard and protect the houses of our souls.

Let us arise each day with the commitment and determination to dedicate ourselves to the proper service of the Holy One Blessed be He, showing our heartfelt appreciation for the gift of our lives by dedicating ourselves each and every day to that day's service. Each day we need to renew and to strengthen our commitment to Torah and mitzvot, to call to our God to guide us and to help us accomplish our important tasks. Without His help and support we may, God forbid, become weak and vulnerable to the nefarious influences and temptations that surround us.

We can see ourselves as peaceful warriors who each day prepare to meet and to vanquish any enemy. Each day brings new battles, and our enemies are cunning and clever. They may not even appear as our enemies, but disguise themselves as our friends or even as our helpers, so we must be vigilant and on our guard. We must protect our precious flames and defend the sanctity of our homes. We cannot allow ourselves to become complacent or lazy. Our enemies take no vacations and will seize any opportunity to divert us from our work, deriving their strength from our weakness. Their existence is predicated on our inattention. Wherever they may gain a new foothold, they act quickly to establish their dominion. When this occurs, God forbid, our ability to repulse their invasion becomes even more difficult, so we must keep our gates closed and be vigilant against any incursion.

When we are tired or weak, we can strengthen ourselves by the knowledge of the great importance of our work, and by yearning to come closer to our King, to feel His loving and protective presence, to bring the light of His holiness into our lives. This goal will motivate us to overcome sloth and to meet the challenge of vanquishing our enemies. With this vision, we can strengthen ourselves and not give in to despair. We must dedicate our houses to the service of our Master. Let us cleanse and purify our houses to receive His light, remembering always the true purpose of our lives.

May God give us the clarity and understanding to recognize our enemies, within and without.

May He grant us the strength to overcome all our foes.

May He guide us and watch over us all the days of our lives. Amen.

# New Beginnings

# Walk Before Me and Be Perfect

Can a man of flesh and blood attain perfection? Is it possible for human beings to make themselves whole and complete? The command was given to Abram to make himself perfect. He was given the commandment to circumcise himself and to walk before God, his source of life.

Abram had separated himself from the prevalent idolatrous belief systems of his time by physically and spiritually distancing himself from the pagan worship that had surrounded him in Aram. God saw that Abram was now ready to take on the responsibility of making himself whole and complete before his Creator. He would now be called Abraham, the father of a multitude of nations.

How can we emulate our father, Abraham? How can we separate ourselves from all the misunderstandings and misconceptions that are to be found in our time? How can we walk before God in wholeness and completeness? Our forefather Abraham blazed the trail and secured the way. He set into place the foundation for his descendants, who would then be able to build a location for God's presence in the world. His children would become the guardians of God's Torah, continuing the work of their forefather by proclaiming the name of the Holy One, Blessed be He, among the nations. Would they be capable of continuing and perpetuating the legacy that they had inherited? Would the children, like their father, be able to find favor in the eyes of their Creator?

Abraham made it possible for his children to follow his example. God recorded in His Torah the events and experiences in the life of His faithful servant to serve as an example for all the generations to come. In every generation, the Children of Abraham have been taught about their righteous forefather, who had the strength and courage to oppose the entire world in order to serve his Master. Abraham taught us, through his words and his actions, the true path that we are to follow in our sojourn through the days of our lives.

Abraham instilled within his children a spiritual inheritance that would last throughout the history of the Jewish people. Because of this inheritance every Jew has the capability of becoming, like him, a true servant of God. Because of his successful efforts in responding to all the tremendous challenges that he faced, his descendants have been imbued with the potential to emulate him. Through the great labor of our forefather Abraham, the great gift of Torah and mitzvot would be passed on to future generations. Through his diligent efforts, his children would be given the opportunity to bring themselves closer to their Creator. Following the path of their father, his children could learn the lessons of true service of their Master.

Is it within our capability to walk before our Creator and to be perfect? Because our forefather Abraham succeeded in meeting all the challenges that he was faced with in his time, his children have within them the capability of successfully meeting all the challenges that they may be faced with in their time. Although the challenges, and the times, may be different, we have, forever, as our spiritual legacy, the capability to respond to them successfully. The Children of Israel, as the spiritual heirs of their righteous forefather, must not abandon the directive given to them by God. We can, and must, strive to make ourselves whole and complete.

God has, throughout Jewish history, given us the mandate to perfect ourselves in his service. He has given the Jewish people His Teachings, His love, and His support. He has watched over us, and guided us, throughout the generations. He has given us teachers and guides to help and to lead us by their righteous example. All that we need to fulfill God's mandate has been provided. Abraham taught us how to successfully meet our challenges. He showed us the path of righteous devotion, imbuing us with his own strength and courage. We, his children, must live up to the standard he set for us. It is the work we have been given to do and have the capability of doing. We must follow the example of Abraham to serve our Master in wholeness, in completeness, in awe, and in love.

# Willows by the Stream

And the time will come when the willows will sprout forth from among the grasses of the earth. They will be watered and nourished by streams of water that will bring life-giving sustenance from their Source. These streams will emanate from their holy Source and provide the land with abundant water to bring new life to the parched earth.

The earth has been dry for a long time and the willows have struggled to sustain themselves with scant resources. The channels of life-giving waters have been stopped up and the earth has struggled to retain its moisture. We have adapted to our thirsty condition and have learned to make do with our meager rations. Although the willows have not been able to flourish as in earlier times, they have managed to grow and to endure. The heartiest plants have been those growing closest to their Source of water. Those thirsty plants that drank up every available drop of water were able to grow despite the scarcity of resources. They clung to their Source of life tenaciously and valued every precious drop.

In fields of dead and dying grass, there could always be seen clusters of green and vibrant life. These hearty willows have stood out in contrast to their peers. The other grasses of the fields did not appreciate the great importance of the streams within their midst and they did not understand the connection between their withered and lifeless condition and their lack of vivifying water. In the past they had had a level of understanding, but over time they became accustomed to their lowly existence, their expectations became diminished and their yearnings suppressed.

Over the years only a few hearty willows have been able to grow and to sustain themselves under these harsh and barren conditions. They recognized their desperate situation and tried to convey their understanding to those around them, but most often their pleas went unheeded.

We must recognize the state of our impoverishment, understanding the great importance of our life-giving spiritual Source of nourishment and sustenance. We must yearn for the rains from above to shower us with heavenly influence and blessing so that the yellowed and withered land will again turn green and vibrant.

The time will come. The promise will be kept. The Source of spiritual beneficence is ready and eager to bestow His blessings. We must dream of lush green meadows of tall green grass and prepare ourselves to receive the refreshing and vivifying waters that will bring renewed life and growth to our parched and thirsty fields.

Following the example of those hearty plants among us that have used their resources wisely and cherished all opportunities to receive replenishment, we must search for the scarce and elusive streams of precious water hidden beneath the earth. We must pray for the end of our drought and for the onset of plentiful and abundant rainfall, may it be soon in our days. Amen.

# In Search of You

I need to feel Your presence in my life, dear Lord. I yearn for the comfort of Your warm and glowing light. When my mind becomes still, I can focus my awareness on You, dear God. When I move away from the distractions around me, I can bring consciousness of You into my heart.

When I open my heart to Your holy Presence dear Lord, I can feel the warmth of Your love and the peace of my soul. When I sit in meditation of Your great glory, dear God, my fears melt away and my concerns become small. I wonder how it is that I allow myself to get caught up in the worries and concerns of the world around me when I know that You are always there behind the scenes directing the course of my life with a true and discerning hand. I need to stop every day, many times each day, to ensure that I keep that knowledge secure in my heart.

Living in the world and keeping an awareness of You can be a daunting task. The many voices that call to me pull me in one direction after another, voices from the present, the past and the future. The different aspects of my being are pulled toward the many attractions that exist in this world. I must stop myself from running after them. I must sit in my place and remind myself of Who my Master is, and Who it is I must keep in my mind always.

When I search for Your Presence, dear God, I feel I am home. When I look to bring You into my heart, I know I am safe from all harm. After I have pushed away all the worries and concerns from my mind, I can then make room for a full and undivided consciousness of my Master. I can come back to myself, my true self. I can sit in my home, my true home. I am in the Presence of my Father, my true Father, and I know that I have nothing to fear.

Please help me, dear God, to keep the awareness of Your Presence in my life always within my heart. Help me, at all times, to be able to recognize Your loving and guiding Hand in my life. My recognition of You keeps me from sin. When I am aware of Your Presence, dear Lord, I am never lost, but can always see the road ahead of me clearly. It is only when I am caught up in the distractions around me that I am prone to losing my way. When my mind and my heart are directed toward You, dear God, the path in front of me becomes clear and illuminated.

I must keep my focus. The evil inclination is a master of confusion, an expert in illusion and falsehood. It is easy to be fooled when we are not careful to guard ourselves against these deceptions and distortions of truth. We can easily be misled when we allow ourselves to wander away from true awareness of our Master.

It is my responsibility to cling to my God and to ensure that my thoughts are directed toward heaven, always keeping the knowledge and truth of Your existence in my mind. I must search for You, and follow You, throughout my days and into my nights. I look to You, dear God, to be my Protector and my Guide, knowing it is only in Your good and merciful ways that I can put my trust.

Please do not forsake Your humble servant, dear God. Please do not leave me unprotected in this world. Please reveal Your illuminating light to this humble and contrite seeker, dear Lord. My soul cries out in longing to cling to her Source. Please allow her the loving comfort and security of Your Presence. May her longings be satisfied, dear God, and may she always be able to find shelter under the wings of Your Protection, now and forever. Amen

# The Caged Bird

Our souls are imprisoned, held captive by our physicality. The bird is restrained within her cage. She longs to fly, to spread her wings and soar gracefully skyward, but alas, within her cage her movement is restricted. Despite her restrictions, however, the graceful bird still retains her love of flying. The beautiful bird has never resigned herself to the state of her captivity. Given the opportunity, she is ever ready to escape her cage and to fly freely. In her heart she retains her strong and vibrant, natural instinct to fly, flapping her wings and moving freely and gracefully through the air.

Her Master has placed her in a confining cage, restricting her movement in a protective but limiting environment. The bird sings her sweet and lovely melodies trying to arouse the attention of her Master to remember her and set her free. Her song vibrates within her small breast, her tiny heart cries out for its freedom.

The beautiful bird will never give up hope of attaining her freedom or relinquishing her dream of escaping her confining cage. She moves around within her cage in readiness and preparation for the door of her liberation to open, holding the promise of liberation securely in her heart. She continues to sing her song and flap her wings in expectation, knowing that one day her loving Master will release her.

We all have inside of us a beautiful bird with the strong inclination to spread her wings and to move heavenward. We all have a sweet and pure voice within us that longs to be heard. Our beautiful birds are often neglected and ignored as we turn a deaf ear to their heartfelt cries and to the plight of their existence.

It was our Master who placed these birds within their cages, but he also gave us the keys necessary to open them. The mitzvot of the Torah are the keys. Whenever we follow the ways of our Master we are giving freedom to our souls by allowing our bird-like spiritual nature to spread her wings. When we heed the beautiful voice from within, we become aware of our true nature and we are then able to unlock our true potential.

Our souls yearn to fly heavenward and our Master yearns to set them free. In His great generosity and magnanimity, He has given us His Torah, the keys to our own redemption. Our freedom is within our grasp. We must remember the plight of the imprisoned bird and feel the sorrow of her imprisonment. We must heed her cries for liberation, and remember our own true nature.

May it be our Master's will to aid and to encourage us in the work of our redemption.

May our Master always provide us with the means to accomplish our goals.

May the skies be filled with free-flying birds soaring heavenward.

# Awaiting the Dawn

In our despair clouds of darkness surround us and the light from above seems distant and unreachable. Our hearts are filled with sorrow when we perceive the distance that stands between us and our salvation. We have accustomed ourselves to our life in exile. We have adapted ourselves to living estranged and separated from the holy presence of our God, of our Temple, and of our land. We have all but forgotten our former status as emissaries of our Master the King and how it came to be that we fell from our exalted position to our current lowly state.

Our minds have become distracted, our hearts have become depressed, but our souls retain the glorious memory of what once existed and what will one day exist again. The truth of our souls cries out to us, telling us that we have never truly been abandoned. Our souls entreat us to look past our current degraded state toward the light and clarity of our future redemption. The voices of our souls implore us to have faith and confidence in the coming of the dawn. We must understand that the current cycle of suffering and estrangement that we are experiencing is due to our own blindness.

We have been the cause of this suffering and estrangement, having placed the barriers that keep us distant from our God. It is we who have weakened ourselves in our steadfast commitment to our Master, allowing the nations of the world to rule over us when we did not follow the rule of our true King. In our darkness we lost our way. One wrong turn led to another and we were no longer able to find our way back. Our King never truly left us, but our own blindness created a distance between us. We have languished over much time in our state of exile and estrangement

and have often despaired of ever finding our way out of our depressed state. We have almost given up hope of ever being saved
from our sorrowful situation.

The soul of the Jewish people has never stopped believing
in the end of the exile and has never lost hope. We have endured
the enmity of the nations time and time again, but we have not
lost our courage or succumbed to the never-ending assaults that
have been lodged against us. Within the Jewish soul has been
retained the strength of our belief and our trust in God's salvation. Despite the clouds of darkness that often enveloped us, we
held fast to the knowledge that we would never be abandoned
by our God. We knew with certainty that deliverance would one
day come. Even though much time has passed since the glorious time when our Temple stood, and when our priests and our
royalty served their King, the collective Jewish soul has persisted
and survived.

Even as other defeated nations have assimilated and disap-
peared into history, the Jewish people have continued to exist. God
had promised us that we would always be under His protection
and care. In His covenant with us we were granted everlasting security that has withstood the many centuries of Jewish existence,
and will continue. The relationship between the Jewish people
and their God will endure. The end of exile and the redemption
of the Jewish people will come about as surely as dawn follows
the darkness of night.

I have faith and confidence in Your protection, dear Lord.
The wisdom of my soul tells me You will never abandon us. I know
that it has only been because of Your great love and concern, that
the Jewish people have survived the darkness of exile and that our
own blindness has caused our suffering. I wait with great trust
and anticipation for Your salvation, dear God, and with faith and
with confidence in the fulfillment of Your promise. Although this
wait has been a long and difficult one, I look forward to the light
of redemption and not backward to the darkness of exile. I wait,

with eager anticipation, for the time to come when we will witness the great revelation of Your holy light.

May it be soon and in our days. Amen

# The Vineyard

The vineyard of God has been uprooted. The good and fertile land stands desolate and uncultivated. This once thriving land has been covered over with thicket and brambles. The great tower has been toppled and the wine vats are in ruins. No grapes issue forth from the scattered vines. The Guardian of the vineyard has distanced Himself from His once flourishing land. He has allowed His possessions to be overrun by strangers who do not know how to bring forth a harvest. The precious land lies barren. The stones of the tower lie in heaps on the ground and the wine vats are broken and empty.

Woe to the once flourishing people who worked diligently for their Master. Their vines were laden with succulent fruit and their vats were overflowing with pure and abundant wine. What happened to the strong and healthy vines that grew forth from this fertile land? Where is the abundant produce that once covered the land from one end to the other?

The vines withered, dried up from lack of life-sustaining water. They could no longer receive the blessings of vitality that had irrigated them from their Source and Protector and they had become disconnected from the channels of their nourishment. Without adequate sustenance the vineyard became parched and dry and could no longer produce its fruit. There were no grapes to press and wine became scarce in the land.

How can we properly sanctify ourselves and bring honor to our Master? We are no longer able to produce the holy wine of sanctification. We are no longer able to provide the pure and abundant produce from which the holy wine was derived. The Master of the vineyard mourns the loss of His most prized possession. He looks sadly at the overrun fields, the broken vats and the idle winepresses and remembers the time when His bounty was overflowing with ripe and succulent fruit. The Master waits with sorrowful patience for the time when He will be able to return to His vineyard. Although He has never forgotten His vineyard, He has had to distance Himself from it. The Master of the vineyard could not dwell in a place of desolation and ruin.

We must restore the lost honor to our Master's vineyard and prepare a proper and fitting place for Him to dwell within the land. We must strive to bring back the vivifying waters from above to rain down once again upon the land, restoring the parched and lifeless vines that have been scattered among the nations. With our love and dedication, we can cause the vineyard of our Master to grow and to flourish once again, transforming a place of desolation into a paradise of life and of growth. The sorrowful estrangement that has distanced us from our Master can be ended.

May we have the merit to bring forth a flow of pure and holy wine to issue from the ripe and nourishing grapes of our Master's vineyard soon in our days. Amen.

# The Children of His House

The children who had grown up under the influence of our forefather Abraham had been imbued with a new understanding. All around them were nations of idol worshippers, but they were privileged to be taught the unique vision of their mentor and guide Abraham. The three hundred and eighteen individuals who were part of the household of Abraham had been given a very different understanding of the true nature of the world. They were taught about one God Who is the creator of everything, Who sustains everything, and Who is responsible for everything past, present, and future. They learned about the true God Who is one, indivisible, and without peer. Although He cannot be seen by the physical eye or understood by the physical brain, He can be seen and understood by the soul that resides within the human being. It was a concept that had been understood by Noah, but had been rejected by most of his descendants.

In Abraham's time, many gods with different powers were believed to be responsible for the diverse and numerous creations within the physical world. The idea of one creator who is responsible for everything seemed strange and illogical to the peoples of that time. The concept that one master could rule over all of existence was beyond their comprehension.

Even as a child, our forefather Abraham had begun to ponder the nature of existence – how it had originated, was maintained, and was perpetuated. He looked around himself and he looked within himself. He searched for the answers that would lead him toward proper understanding. He yearned to know who his Creator was, and how he could make a connection to Him. In order for Abraham to realize his life's purpose, he needed to know who his Master was and how he should serve Him. He understood that there was meaning to existence and he was determined to discover it.

Abraham set a new course, giving the world a true understanding of God and of the duties of humankind. Despite the fact that he stood almost alone within his generation, Abraham had discovered the truth and he did not compromise his beliefs. He spread his message, taught his initiates and imbued them with his clear vision of God and of humankind.

Those children who grew up in the house of Abraham were privileged to hear their master's teachings. They were taught to recognize the one true Source of blessing from Whom all life flows and to discover and to know their own souls. They learned how to live their lives, and Who it is they must always serve. They understood that their teacher's guidance would lead them on the proper path, and that under his loving direction their lives would be fulfilled and meaningful. Their God would take pride in their accomplishments, and their days would be blessed.

We are the children of our father Abraham. We, like the children nurtured in his house, can study the life and accomplishments of our great ancestor and emulate his ways. Just as he searched to find God, we must search for Him. Just as he discovered his holy soul, we must discover our holy souls. Just as he dedicated his life to serving God, we must dedicate our lives to God's service. We must follow the direction and guidance of our forefather Abraham, to cleave to the truth of Torah and to be steadfast in our service to our God, the Holy One Blessed be He.

# Trapped Within the Ice

When something freezes it becomes motionless and static, unable to grow or to develop. Whatever its condition at the moment it becomes frozen will remain its condition until exposed to a source of heat. This describes the physical state of freezing and thawing. But there is a spiritual counterpart to these processes.

Physical heat is generated by the sun and by the heat of molten lava within the earth's core. Heat comes both through a source above us and a source hidden beneath us inside the earth. Similarly, in a spiritual sense, we have a source of heat generated from above and one that is generated from a hidden source inside. Heat is an essential element in the cycle of life. We know that a cold, frozen planet cannot sustain life; so too, in a state of spiritual frozenness, life cannot be sustained. Just as God has given us the sun to keep us physically alive, He has given us the Torah as the Source of heat and light to sustain our spiritual beings.

Our interior source of heat comes from the flame of our souls. By feeding and enriching the flame inside us with the light of Torah and mitzvot, we are able to utilize the life-sustaining heat from our God. When, God forbid, we turn away from the light source of our Torah, the flame inside becomes encased in ice and blocks the invigorating, internal light from generating its spiritual life-sustaining warmth. Such a condition puts us, God forbid, in a state of alienation from both our inner source of light and our outer Source.

Darkness causes confusion; coldness causes stagnation. These elements are the tools of evil used to keep us from serving our God. When our souls are encased within frozen barriers, we become lost to our God and also to our true selves. In such a state we cannot grow and develop spiritually and our negative inclinations are given free rein. When we cut ourselves off from our life-sustaining Source, we become unable to withstand the numerous and omnipresent negative influences that thrive in cold and dark environments. We weaken our spiritual immune systems when we remove ourselves from our Source of light. Our ability to discern and comprehend the dangers becomes diminished. Over time we become accustomed to living in our dark and cold environments as the ice forms layers around our inner flames.

Although the ice can form barriers around our souls, it cannot extinguish the flames. Our spiritual lights can be isolated and even estranged but not eradicated. As long as we are physically alive we can, through the process of repentance, melt the accumulated ice, no matter how hard or thick it has become. By assimilating the light of mitzvot, by establishing and maintaining a connection to our Source of heat and light, and by expressing heartfelt regret and sorrow for having allowed ourselves to move so far from the light, we can cause the hardest and thickest ice to melt.

We must connect ourselves to holiness and bask in the rays of God's golden sunshine, to warm ourselves by the glow of His teachings, and to sit in places illuminated by Torah. Thoughts of praise and thanksgiving must have a place to dwell in our hearts and to be spoken by our lips. We must avail ourselves of all opportunities to bring ourselves closer to the Source of all that we have and all that we are. Our spiritual existence and survival depends on our efforts to connect to our life-Source.

No one can do this work for us. If we neglect our responsibilities, we are putting our lives in jeopardy. There will be no one else to blame. We must wake up to the call of our souls' voices. They are pleading with us to free them from their icy prisons, longing to spread their light and influence to enliven and illuminate us, and yearning to connect to their Source. Listen to their cries. Do not turn away from these pleas. Do not turn deaf ears to their loving admonitions.

Begin today to melt the accumulations of ice surrounding

your soul. Even if your progress is slow and uneven, do not give up or despair of achieving your goal. Every particle of ice that melts will bring us closer to the great light of our Master and to His loving protection, guidance, and care. We must remain focused on our goal and make it our lives' work.

May our efforts be successful in the eyes of our Creator. Amen.

# Transformation

When we engage ourselves in communication with our Creator, we do so with the idea that we will be able to affect Him. Like a penitent pleading for forgiveness, or a patient asking for a cure, we come before our Creator with requests that we hope will influence Him to favor us with those things that we feel we are lacking. Although such requests are proper and necessary, it is not really God Who will, or Who needs to be, influenced. Since He knows what our needs are better than we do, why do we need to ask?

When we stand before our God we must leave behind our false pride and our sense of self-sufficiency. We must come before the Holy One, Blessed be He, as paupers who are completely dependent on their benefactor. Everything we have or have ever received has come from His hand. We must remember that our own efforts or expertise are not responsible for our livelihood whenever we come before our God in prayer. Our egos have no place in this communication.

We must come before our Creator knowing that every breath we take, and every piece of bread that has been given into our hands, has been given to us by our God. Our survival in every moment of time is dependent on His beneficence. Before we open our lips to utter a word of prayer, we must acknowledge that we are standing in front of our Creator and Benefactor Who constantly sustains our lives.

When we approach our God in prayer we need to shed our many identities. We are no longer businesspeople, teachers, doctors, parents or children, but rather the creations of our Creator. We are the handiwork that He has fashioned, creations granted the gift of life. We are not independent, self-sufficient or self-made, but wholly dependent on our Father the King.

The prerequisite to proper prayer is to divest ourselves of all illusions that we ever could accomplish anything without the help and approval of our Creator. We must come before our God with humility and with trust. We should not ask for the desires of our egos, but rather for the understanding to be able to fulfill the desires of our Master. We need to be educated to know in what direction we are meant to travel and be guided on how best to accomplish the work we are meant to do.

When we stand before our Creator we must open our hearts to His will, to that work which He has assigned to us. We must come before Him as loyal servants ready and willing to serve our Master, to understand and fulfill His implicit directives as well as His explicit ones.

Show me the way, dear God. Direct me to my proper path. Please keep me from distractions and from laziness. Please keep me alert both to the opportunities and to the obstacles that I may find along my path. Help me to understand the assignments I am given and strengthen me in my determination to accomplish them to the best of my ability. Help me to use all the gifts of life that you have bestowed on Your humble servant to serve You in truth and with purpose.

You know, dear God, what my needs are. You know what mission I am here to accomplish, the purpose and meaning of my life and of all life. Help me to understand what You want so that I can serve you appropriately and to the best of my ability. I ask for good health in order to serve You. I ask for sustenance, clothing and shelter in order to serve You. I ask for a spouse to help me to serve you and for children whom I can teach to serve You. I ask for the wisdom to recognize the forces of evil and the strength in order to be able to withstand their power. I ask for Your forgiveness when I forget Your Torah and succumb to their persuasiveness.

When we finish speaking to God, we should not come away

from this meeting feeling that we have influenced or affected Him, but rather, that this encounter has influenced and affected us. Prayer, if it is to be effective, must be an experience of transformation.

In our prayer we must open our hearts and our minds as well as our ears, to God's voice, making ourselves receptive to His words, to His guidance and to His direction. We must be willing to go in directions and to do work that may be beyond our comprehension. Like our father Abraham, who rose up early to do the will of His Creator, fulfilling commands he could not understand, we must follow his example to accomplish our God's directives even when they may be puzzling to our limited understanding. The time we spend in communication with our Creator should be used wisely and with great appreciation for the opportunity of this meeting. By using the time we spend in communication with our Creator wisely, we demonstrate our appreciation for the great opportunity of this meeting.

May you have the merit to understand the lessons you have been given to learn.

May you be able to take the inspiration you have gained through your prayers and be mindful of it throughout your day.

May you leave this meeting renewed and strengthened in your commitment to serve your Creator with all your heart, with all your soul and with all your resources. Amen.

# Birds in Flight

To stay airborne birds cannot simply glide across the sky but must constantly flap their wings. They must continuously expend energy in order to reach their destination. We understand this simple principle of flight as it pertains to birds, but there is also a lesson for us to learn. If we seek to elevate ourselves and get closer to our God, we must constantly and consistently expend our energy; as soon as we stop flapping our wings, we begin our descent.

We tend to view our lives as compartmentalized, separating the physical and the spiritual aspects. We may think that serving God is reserved for the time we spend in synagogue, or for special times like Shabbat and holidays. However, the Torah teaches that all human endeavors should be in the service of God. We primarily look at ourselves as physical beings and, only secondarily, as spiritual beings, yet the truth of our existence is just the opposite.

We are, first and foremost, spiritual beings. Our physical bodies are the means that enable us to function, but they are not our true identities. When we view ourselves as physical beings we are grossly underestimating our true worth and capabilities. If we limit ourselves to our animal functions, then, indeed, we resemble animals. If, instead, we view ourselves and behave like spiritual beings, we then resemble angels.

Angels are spiritual beings who exist to praise, honor and serve their Creator; this is also the true work of human beings. For angels this work is done in a spiritual realm where recognition of the Creator is apparent. Human beings, however, must work in an environment where the truth of spiritual existence is not readily apparent. The location may be different, but the work is the same – to praise, honor and serve our Creator.

The root of the Hebrew word for world is *olam* which means hidden. To do the spiritual work of angels in an environment of hidden spirituality is our great challenge. Like the flying birds, our work involves continuous effort and attention. If we do not constantly remind ourselves of our true identities, and the underlying truth of our existence, we stop flapping our wings and quickly become earthbound. We must maintain a constant awareness of our spiritual beings, constantly searching to find the spirituality hidden within our world, thereby liberating the sparks of holy light that have been encased in the physical environment of impurity since the sin of Adam and Eve.

Allowing the great light of spirituality to become manifest reverses the process that sin has caused. With the guidance and direction of the Torah we can undo sin's damage and perfect the world in God's service. We have the opportunity and responsibility to do this work every moment of every day of our lives and it requires our best efforts to be accomplished. Since the time of Adam and Eve, it has been the mandate of human existence to expend effort and energy to repair the damage caused by our ancestors.

Our work is of great importance and requires diligence. Each of us is given the awesome responsibility of rectifying the effects of generations of individual, as well as collective, sins. We must work to repair damage done in the past and strive to perfect ourselves in the present. In so doing, we can create connections of spiritual influence that can positively affect our environment.

To do this work effectively requires our dedication and our perseverance, keeping our eyes trained on our destination and our wings constantly flapping. We must take care to avoid complacency or resting on past achievements. We were placed here by our Creator to work with Him to transform our dense and dark physical environment into one of spiritual light and clarity. We must recognize and accept the position we have been given, appreciate its importance, and work with all our spiritual and physical resources to achieve these goals.

May our efforts be faithful.

May our resolve remain strong.

May our achievements find favor in the eyes of our Creator. Amen.

# Boundaries

During a flood the sea overflows its boundaries causing damage to the land. When the sea stays within its boundaries, it is beneficial to the land, but when it overruns the shore it can cause great destruction. This dynamic can also be applied to human relationships. When we stay within our boundaries in our relationships with others, the result will be mutually beneficial and enriching, but when we allow our egos to trespass their proper boundaries, great damage can occur.

It is the nature of our negative inclinations to take from others, and to exert influence over others and even control others. Our egos' weaknesses create a desire for dominance in order to feed on the energy of others, thereby making them vulnerable to the designs of our negativity. The strength of our spiritual natures, however, works in quite the opposite way. Our souls want to give to others and they yearn to enrich, to enlighten and to spread their positive, loving essence to those who are receptive to their Godly influence

Our negative inclinations are like the bullies who try to gain power and dominance by intimidation. When not tempered by the positive influence of the soul, the ego is inclined toward aggression and dominance that is rooted in its feelings of fear and insecurity. When the ego is not firmly connected to its spiritual being, it feels lost and vulnerable.

To compensate for these feelings of inadequacy, the ego tries to exert its power over others in order to feel a sense of security, however temporary and superficial. The ego's reasoning derives from its false understanding of its own importance in relation to others. Under the influence of the negative inclination, the ego believes that if it can control others then it must be strong and powerful. The ego acts like a thief who steals, and who has to continue stealing in order to remind himself of his false power. It is a strategy that appears successful, but in reality only further weakens the ego's true level of security and influence.

True strength, power and security can only be obtained by aligning ourselves with the Holy One, Blessed be He. The human ego is vulnerable and limited. Without an alliance with its spiritual partner the soul, its existence is tenuous and fragile. When a person aligns himself with his spiritual nature, he grows in authentic strength, the strength of goodness, love, care and concern. Although it may appear as if the giving person is losing and the taking person is gaining, in reality just the opposite is occurring. By giving of ourselves to others we are strengthening our connections with others as well as our connection to the great spiritual power of our Master, the pre-eminent Giver.

When we try to take by bullying and force, it is a demonstration of weakness. When we feel the need to control and dominate, it is an expression of our fears and insecurities. In our insecurity we try to attach ourselves to the energy of others to create the illusion of importance and security. We mistakenly believe we can take from others what we feel lacking in ourselves. When we allow our egos to overrun their boundaries, we diminish ourselves, causing our own spiritual depletion. In striving to make ourselves appear intimidating and powerful we can, God forbid, become cut off from our true Source of power, becoming truly weak and helpless.

We must recognize our boundaries and not allow the aggressive tendencies of a weak ego cause harm to others, developing an appreciation for the beauty and goodness that resides in every soul. Although that goodness may not be readily apparent, we are obligated to search for the spiritual greatness hidden within everyone. When we focus on the positive traits of others, our own spirituality becomes enhanced. By looking for and discovering the goodness in others, we can make them more aware of their own goodness.

When we value and show appreciation for the spiritual growth and achievements of others, we foster that growth in ourselves as well. When we make others the recipients of our love and care, they will generally respond with love and care. For some individuals who have been badly hurt by the aggression and dominance of others, the process of healing and loving may take time, but we should not get discouraged. Just as drops of soft water can eventually penetrate hard rock, so too can soft words of love penetrate a hurt and hardened heart.

No efforts to be loving, caring and respectful are ever exerted in vain. Even if others do not respond to our kindness, the giving will always enrich us. There are no limitations on our access to the storehouse of spiritual goodness. Our Source of spiritual bounty is infinite. The spiritual equation teaches us that to take is to lose and to give is to gain. The sea of our egos must be disciplined to stay within its boundaries. The land around us must be allowed to grow and develop without our interference. We must guard and control the desires of the ego and respect the boundaries of others. We must never cause damage, but instead bring healing love and soulful consciousness to all our interactions with others in the name of our great Healer, Benefactor and Source of goodness in the world, the Holy One, Blessed be He. Amen.

# The Seed

The seed is placed carefully in the fertile soil where it will break down from its original shape and be transformed to a sprout of new life. This sprout must be nourished and replenished with nutrients derived from the earth, the water and the sun. The earth represents the material state of the world, the water represents Torah knowledge and the sun represents God's light. Human beings, of earthly origin, can be transformed through their Torah study and to their adherence to mitzvot and prayer.

The seed of this transformation exists in all of us, but in order to develop, the seed must change. The growth and development of the seed is dependent on our own efforts to nurture and cultivate it; it cannot occur through stagnation. The fully mature blossoming flower does not resemble the seed in its original state.

Each of us has the ability to blossom into a beautiful flower whose petals open toward the sun. Although the flower is planted firmly in the earth, it grows toward the sky attracted by the life-giving rays of the sun. We are our own gardeners and are responsible for the growth and the maturation of our potential. It is our responsibility to nourish ourselves with the waters of Torah and reach toward the light of our God.

We have been blessed with fertile earth. All that we need to reach our potential has been provided. Each of us will develop different kinds of stems, leaves and flowers based on the specific seed. We need not compare or wish for a different seed or a different plot of earth in which to develop. Our Creator, in His infinite wisdom, placed our particular seed in its best location and provided it with all its necessities for growth. We have been given all that we require to blossom into healthy, beautiful flowers that reflect the great wisdom and beneficence of our Creator.

The potential has been provided, the means of nourishment are plentiful and the waters of Torah are unceasing. It is our responsibility to drink from these waters and to reach toward this light. Our God provides us with our material needs as well as our spiritual requirements. By recognizing the benefits available to us we can make proper use of them. We must accept the events and circumstances of our lives as our allotted portion. If, God forbid, we complain or reject these circumstances, we are asserting our false pride above the infinite wisdom of our Creator, Blessed be He.

By removing all traces of arrogance and by accepting our role in the divine plan, we can open our hearts to His love, His teachings and His commands. These are the essential nutrients of our spiritual growth and the ways that our seeds can break through the boundaries of our earthly existence and grow toward the illuminating light of heaven. This process is neither easy to understand nor to accomplish, but the results of our labor will bring us the joy of closeness to our God and the great benefit of His love and care.

There is no goal in heaven or on earth that can compare to this achievement. It is the true meaning and purpose of our lives; all other joys and accomplishments are like nothing by comparison. To know that we are doing our Master's assignments to the best of our abilities, is in itself the greatest reward. When we strive toward the goal of self-perfection, we bring joy to our Father in Heaven. When the goals of spiritual growth that He has set for us are achieved to their utmost capability, we are then accomplishing the purpose of all creation.

Join me my friend. Become your own gardener. Work lovingly and diligently every day in your Father's garden. Allow the great potential of your seed to develop itself into the strong, beautiful and holy flower that it is capable of becoming. Water your sprout well with the waters of Torah, nourish it with mitzvot, and watch the seed of your soul blossom, reflecting the holy light of heaven.

# The Never-Ending Battle

The nature of evil is parasitic, feeding on the negativity of human behavior. The more spiritually developed we become; the less ability evil has to find sustenance. When we, God forbid, turn away from our God, and from the teachings of His Torah, we allow ourselves to become hosts to negative forces. Conversely, when we involve ourselves in Torah, mitzvot, and in following God's ways, evil has no place to which to become attached. The best defense against the forces of negativity is the offense of Torah.

Our involvement in spiritual pursuits naturally leads to greater attachment to God. When we are connected to Him, evil has no chance to gain a foothold. As long as we nourish ourselves with the holy nourishment of Torah and mitzvot, evil has no place from which to feed. In attaching ourselves to God, we become conduits for His influence in the world, becoming channels for the manifestation of our Creator's blessings. Our efforts increase the light of holiness and negate the efforts of evil. We are continually presented with this awesome responsibility and its inherent challenges.

The ongoing conflict between good and evil exists internally within human beings and externally between human beings, between us and our environments, between us and our God. Just as a rock thrown into a lake will cause many ripples, so too do our thoughts, words and actions have many effects both internally and externally. A mitzvah not only brings good into existence, it also brings good into the doer of the mitzvah. Unfortunately the reverse is true as well. Our negative behaviors can bring negativity within us as well as around us, allowing evil to thrive. A place that can nurture great holiness can also be a host to great evil; they cannot, however, coexist.

We need to appreciate the gifts we are given and to use them to the best of our abilities in the service of our Master. Our talents and abilities are the tools we are given to serve our Creator. The greater the strengths that we possess, the greater the potential for channeling the influence of God or, God forbid, for generating evil. For those who have been blessed with greater potential, the challenges of using these gifts for benefit and not, God forbid, for damage is formidable. For such individuals the ability to generate greater holiness is counterbalanced by a correspondingly greater ability to generate evil. All individuals, however, no matter what their level of ability can make a significant difference in the balance of good and evil in the world.

There is no middle ground. A thought, word or action can either be derived from a holy source or an unholy one. Our motivation can either be pure in the name of God or, God forbid, nourished from the forces of impurity. The more we strengthen and develop our positive inclinations, the harder the forces of evil work to distract us and to influence us to abandon our proper paths. For those who are weak in their commitment to Torah values, the negative inclination does not have to exert its full strength. For those, however, who are strong in their commitment to Torah values, the forces of evil need to extend their greatest efforts.

We should never become complacent; the battle between good and evil is ongoing and fierce and there can only be one victor. No matter what has previously been accomplished, we can never rest from this conflict. The battle goes on from within and without; it is fought on many fronts, it has many faces. Past victories will not guarantee future success.

Every day brings new challenges, schemes and strategies from our enemies. We must prepare ourselves to recognize them and respond to them with courage and conviction. Even if we have, unfortunately, been defeated by a particular challenge, we must encourage and strengthen ourselves to engage our adversary again and again until we achieve victory.

Understand well the importance of this struggle. Know what

it is you are fighting for and that it is within your capability to be successful. You are a soldier in the legion of your Master and He has given you the privilege of defending and glorifying His name. Recognize and appreciate this opportunity and do not turn away from your responsibility. Although the work may be difficult, its rewards are abundant.

You can be a conduit for God's blessing or, God forbid, cause blockage of His holy light. The choice is yours to make in every moment of life. May your choices be for blessing and may your Master be pleased with your accomplishments. Amen.

# Elul



*I am for my Beloved and my Beloved is for me*

Dear God, in the month of Elul You give us the gift of closeness to You. The greatest of opportunities is ours at this time, but we do not often show our appreciation by using this gift wisely. The closer we are to You, the greater our clarity of vision and the greater the ability our souls have to generate their illuminating presence.

The benefits of this time are innumerable but the most important of all our opportunities is that of repenting and being forgiven. You are there, dear God, to listen, to help and to guide us in this most important work. As long as we are weighed down with the heaviness of our sins, we cannot lift our feet from their earthly attachments. We become bound to material desire and worthless pursuits, becoming strangers to our souls and distanced from You. In our confusion, we mistake our priorities and expend our energies in directions that yield only temporary rewards.

Elul is a time of opportunity to wake up and recognize our true selves and determine what is in need of rectification. It is a time for reflection and examination in order to prepare our hearts for repentance in the month of Tishray. To do any job properly requires preparation. Elul is a time to open our hearts in honesty to our improper thoughts, speech and actions. With open eyes, we must look and evaluate our misdeeds whether they occurred in our relationship with You or in our relationship with others. Words move quickly from our minds to our lips, too often expressed without sensitivity or deliberation. Actions may be taken without reflection or pause. When we don't take the time to evaluate the propriety of our speech and action, we are bound to repeat inappropriate behavior.

Dear God, in Elul You make Yourself more accessible to us, aiding us in our honest evaluations. You can help us see clearly and objectively in order to understand how far from the true path we have traveled. We must sincerely appeal to You and willingly face the ugliness and shame of our deeds with heartfelt courage and conviction to move far from them. We must yearn to distance ourselves from everything that keeps us from properly serving You. We must have remorse for the negativity and damage we have caused, and firmly resolve to avoid such behavior in the future.

It is only when we acknowledge and take responsibility for our sins that we can take the proper steps to correct them. Although looking critically at our own misdeeds can be painful, it is a process that must not be avoided. Before we can hope to make a true and permanent rectification, we must feel sorrow and shame for our improper behavior.

Dear God, in Elul, You extend Your merciful help. You respond to the broken hearts of Your misguided servants. We understand that to succeed in our work of repentance we need Your firm and loving direction and guidance. We know You will make Yourself available to those who call to You with sincere desire to repent and to go forward in proper service.

Please, dear God, give us the strength and resolve to make the best use of Your closeness at this time. Help us to appreciate the great kindness that You extend to Your children. Help us, dear God, to open our eyes to our sins so that we may ask forgiveness from You and from anyone we may have wronged. Let us view our wrongs with sorrowful eyes and may our hearts feel the pain of the damage we have caused. It is only by feeling this pain that we can strengthen ourselves to avoid repeating our damaging behaviors.

Through our contrite and regretful confessions, may our

prayers for forgiveness be answered, dear God. May the introspection and examination we do in the month of Elul lead us to freedom from our bondage to sin. May our hearts be cleansed of impurity and filled instead with the love, joy and gratitude of knowing that, with Your help and guidance, we have successfully repaired the damage that caused us to be distanced from You. May we appreciate, dear God, the great kindness of Your forgiveness and be steadfast in our resolve not to repeat the sins of the past.

May we be able to look past the regret and sorrow we feel over our past sins and anticipate the joy of serving You properly and wholeheartedly. May the promise of that joy motivate us to do the difficult but essential work of repentance.

May our efforts be sincere and determined.

May our repentance be complete.

May we rejoice in our dedicated and devout service of You.

# Starting Over

A new chapter, a new beginning, a new time freed from attachment to pain, negativity and anger. No longer constrained and powerless before any wave of disturbance or difficulty that threatens to knock you over and toss you about. You have become like a rock firmly embedded in the fertile soil of belief, faith and trust in your Creator. You know that such waves can come at any time, but you also know that you are no longer a helpless pebble that can easily be dislodged.

Joy now fills the places within you where darkness and despair were formerly embedded. The light of your soul and the lights of spirituality that surround you can now be experienced. Your place in the world has been found, and you understand your capabilities and responsibilities more clearly. You feel humbled and strengthened by your understanding of human possibilities and limitations. Although the distance between you and your Creator is great, you know He can be close by your side.

You are thankful for the gift of life, and rejoice at having the opportunities to serve your Master. By using this gift to the best of your ability, you demonstrate your gratitude. No longer stuck in pain, hurt, bitterness and resentment, your heart is now open to love, caring, compassion and acceptance. You understand that we are all connected to one another and that all differences are superficial. Our commonality is our humanity. We can understand the feelings of others based on our own experiences. When we share in the joy and pain of others, we form bonds of love and caring that diminish our differences and enhance our capacity to love.

Your hurt and pain no longer isolate you. You have been liberated from your prison of bitterness and resentment. The reasons that underlie the events and circumstances of your life are beyond your understanding, but you are aware that all of them have contributed to the person you have become. It is your responsibility to imbue your unique role with meaning and purpose. Together with the challenges, help and encouragement came from your Father allowing you to respond to these challenges. At times you became stuck in your sorrow and despair; it was hard to see beyond the pain and confusion of the present and the future seemed shrouded in darkness.

Your God lifted you from your gloom and gave you reason to hope. Holding fast to your hope, you tenaciously clung to life despite the clouds that surrounded you. Your goal was survival, but you received much more. Healed from the traumas and terrors of the past, you can now experience life with a full heart and a glad soul. You have been transformed into a vessel, able to receive blessing from your Lord's bounty and the spiritually nourishing influence of His beneficence. The barriers of negativity have been removed allowing the light within you to shine forth unimpeded. It is your responsibility to keep the channels clear and open within yourself.

Differences have diminished in importance as unity has become predominant. The voice of negativity has been quieted as the positive voice has gained strength and clarity. With the knowledge that your determined efforts to stay on your path will lead you closer to your God, you have become steadfast in your commitment. You have become increasingly diligent in fulfilling the assignments He has given you as you have grown in strength and stability. The successful accomplishment of these responsibilities is your most important goal. Whenever you might be tempted to stray from your path, you must remember this goal and Who it was Who sent you on your appointed mission.

It is a new beginning, a time of rectification and healing of old wounds. That which was crooked has been made straight. That which was broken has been repaired. The chains of attachment to the negativity to the past have been broken. It is time to acknowledge a new day, with new opportunities for a new you.

May the wisdom you have gained in your travels serve you well.

May the truth of the Torah always be your guide.

May your Master be pleased with your accomplishments. Amen.

# The Power of Love

Love is like the brook that gives life to the tree. The waters of love bring forth life and growth. Anger and misunderstanding are like destructive fires that ravage everything in their paths. A tree cut off from its source of water will wither and eventually die; human beings cut off from their loving hearts will become depressed and lose hope. The joy of life is lost to those who are incapable of feeling and expressing love.

To be receptive to the bounty of love is to feel the life source through every pore of one's being. Like the roots of a thirsty tree, we must absorb the life-giving flow to keep ourselves healthy. The invigorating flow of love is the generator of creative energy and emotional growth. When the channels of the heart become blocked, constriction occurs, causing feelings of apathy and depression. Our ability not only to give love, but also to receive love, is crucial to the proper and healthy functioning of our souls.

The positive energy of love is the most potent force in the universe. No star can outshine the radiance of a single loving heart. When one heart opens up to another, a root of love is formed that, over time, grows into a strong and firmly planted tree. Such a tree will be able to withstand winds and rains, because its roots are connected to the most powerful of forces.

When the flow of love is constricted, alienation can occur, creating barriers between us and our souls, between us and our God, and between us and others. Human beings can become robots that function in routine and mechanical ways, yet are disconnected from their feelings. It is our hearts that allow us to make spiritual connections. When our ability to love is impaired, our bodies become shells devoid of their essence and vitality.

It is impossible to truly serve God when we are so constricted that we become, God forbid, cut off from the Source of all life and growth. We can become so attached to our anger, bitterness and negativity that we refuse to relinquish our grasp, holding firmly to those barriers that keep us from spiritual freedom and health. Instead of connecting to our Source of nourishment, we cling to the negative elements that keep us in a state of spiritual, psychological and physical illness and we become our own worst enemies.

We feel entitled to our bitterness and connected to our pain. We weave a web of darkness, cutting ourselves off from the light of love. We feel justified in being the agents of our own diminishment when we choose to focus on negativity and deficiencies, rather than the positive and life-sustaining energy of love. Once we have established a path for ourselves, we either travel toward the warmth and light of love, or God forbid, toward the isolation of anger and resentment.

When we choose negativity, we move away from all that is nourishing to our souls and bring ourselves to a state of spiritual deprivation. When the flames of our souls are dimmed, the ability of our bodies to function becomes impaired. The light of our souls cannot generate its heat and we become estranged from our feelings and alienated from our true selves.

We must recognize this state of illness and work to keep the channels of life-sustaining love open and flowing. We must allow the potent energy of love to invigorate us. We need to become conduits for the radiance of love to nourish and influence everyone and everything around us. One loving heart can bring much joy and light, dispelling darkness and negativity. Each loving heart can uplift and affect the hearts of others. Loving is contagious and its truth can effect great healing, lifting up even the most downcast of souls.

Love is the God-given generating force that invigorates and enlivens our world. It is a powerful instrument for growth and development available to everyone. When we connect our hearts in love and service to our Creator, we transform ourselves and become agents dispersing the holy energy of Godliness in the world. We become true servants of our Master when we mend hearts and bring them closer to their Source.

May our souls rejoice in the light of their Creator.

May the illness of despair be banished from our hearts.

May we join together to unify the great name of our Father in heaven with love and devotion, now and always. Amen.

# About the Author

From the time of her childhood, Cheryl Gunsher has liked to draw and to make up stories. She also spent her early years praying to God, observing the world around her and contemplating its many mysteries. She looked inward as well as outward, channeling her thoughts, feelings and understandings into stories and artwork as well as music and dance. Her childhood interests have continued on throughout the years and she still uses these forms of expression to explore, to understand and to deepen her life's experience.